The Velocity of Money

George Garvy and Martin R. Blyn

Federal Reserve Bank of New York

20424

Second Printing, Revised March 1970

COPIES OF THIS BOOK are available from the Publications Department, Federal Reserve Bank of New York, New York, N. Y. 10045, at $1.50 per copy. Educational institutions may obtain quantities for classroom use at 75 cents per copy.

Library of Congress Catalog Card Number 77-101695

Foreword

M R. GARVY's "Deposit Velocity and its Significance", which was published by the Federal Reserve Bank of New York in 1959, has been out of print for some time. What had started out as an updating of the original booklet led to a completely revised monograph which embodies some of the continuing research on monetary economics going forward at the Federal Reserve Bank of New York.

Since 1959, important developments have taken place in the monetary process as a result of an interaction of rising opportunity costs of money and of advances in cash-saving techniques. Even more radical technological changes in payments mechanisms are being widely discussed. Also, quantitative and other research on the relationship between monetary and real processes has advanced considerably in the decade since the publication of Mr. Garvy's booklet. The present volume, the result of a collaboration by Mr. Garvy and Professor Martin R. Blyn of California State College, Dominguez Hills, reviews and evaluates recent developments with respect to the velocity of money in the light of the new experience and knowledge.

ALFRED HAYES
President

New York City
October 1969

Acknowledgments

The authors wish to acknowledge the unfailing assistance of Miss Abigail M. Cantwell, who edited the manuscript, prepared it for the printer, and saw it through the press. Mr. Thomas Draper helped with the initial editing, Mr. Patrick P. Kildoyle prepared the tables, Miss Evelyn Katz checked the tables and all the references, Messrs. John H. Hendrickson and Sigurds Vidzirkste prepared the charts, and the Misses Kirsti Laandi and Margaret Riebel deserve particular credit for patient typing of the successive drafts.

Contents:

CHARTS

TABLES

1. Introduction

There are many ways of looking at the role of money in our economy. One important facet of monetary analysis is the relationship of income to the stock of money —the velocity of money. The relationship between cash balances and the flow of income or total payments may be defined and measured in a variety of ways, but both theory and experience suggest that the relationship is not stable. The money supply may change significantly, while the flow of income or the volume of payments associated with it remains almost unchanged; the reverse may also occur. The resulting changes in the velocity of money are of considerable interest to analysts as well as to policy makers.

Indeed, changes in the rate of money turnover may be as significant in determining policies intended to achieve appropriate levels of spending as the quantity of money itself, however measured. The historical record shows, for instance, that the occurrence of a 0.2 point increase from one year to another (e.g., from 4.4 to 4.6) in the rate of income velocity is by no means exceptional.[1] Such an increase would be equivalent to an expansion in the stock of money[2] of approximately 4 percent (or roughly $7 billion in 1968).

Since holders of cash can adjust their holdings—allowing for delays, frictions, and inertia—to changes in flows, the demand for cash balances has been the subject

---

[1] *As occurred between 1966 and 1967.*

[2] *For reasons given in Chapter 2, we prefer a definition of money limited to currency in the hands of the public and demand deposits, except interbank and United States Government deposits.*

of many empirical studies of the monetary process. The question of the stability of the relationship of income flows to the stock of money is of particular significance in assessing alternative objectives for, and efficiency in, the conduct of monetary policy. The relationship is very complex for income as well as transactions velocity of money. To be significant, its analysis must go beyond interpretation of statistical data.

Because money serves several distinct functions, changes in the money stock in relation to the flow of goods and services or to the total volume of payments may be traced to influences on the demand for money as a means of payment and for other functions. One of the difficulties in analyzing the money stock is that the demand for money balances is determined not only by economic motives, which can be rationalized or at least categorized in terms of theory, but also by purely technical factors, which affect the efficiency of making payments, locally and at distant points. Over the years, the technology of the payments mechanism has been subject to gradual changes as well as to innovations. These innovations have resulted in rearrangements of payments procedures and related changes in the average stock of money required to accommodate a given flow of payments.

Velocity, however measured, is a statistical averaging of money which moves with money that is mostly at rest and which is held for liquidity and other purposes rather than as a means of payment. The demand for money balances for liquidity purposes will affect velocity independently of the volume of payments for current output and of financial (assets) transactions. Although demand for liquidity itself is related, in a complex manner, to the level of economic activity, it is not necessarily related to its *current* level alone or to the levels of interest rates associated with such activity. The demand for money, as one form of liquidity, is in turn influenced by anticipation of future requirements and by the relative attractiveness of competing liquidity instruments. Thus, velocity of money and of demand deposits, its main component, is influenced by changes in the demand for liquid assets and by the extent to which such demand is satisfied by holding assets other than money. The almost continuous rise in velocity after World War II reflects the diminishing role of money as a means of liquidity and its more efficient use as a means of payment.

Indeed, changes in technology relevant to the function of money as a means of payment are paralleled by changes in the options open to holders of money as a supply of liquidity. These options are continuously affected by changes in the relative attractiveness, in terms of yields offered and risks attached, of various alternative instruments of liquidity or repositories of savings. Such changes are rooted in fluctuations in business and credit conditions as well as in the usual institutional frictions and time lags involved in the spread of innovations. In particular, post-World War II changes in velocity cannot be understood without taking into account innovations in instruments and processes, changes in legal and institutional arrangements, and holder attitudes and preferences.

Thus, one of the reasons for change in the velocity of money over time must be sought in the whole range of conditions and forces that alter the position of money in relation to other liquidity instruments and other means of accumulating financial assets, as well as in relation to those forces that influence demand for payments purposes. Some of the longer run forces, such as the growth of our economy and the rise in the price level since World War II, affect—though not necessarily in the same way—both these main demands. But, while demand for money as a financial asset is best discussed in terms of portfolio balance, the demand for transactions balances is also influenced by purely institutional and technological factors.

All this has not been ignored. Many writers acknowledge such influences, and others at least footnote them properly. Published research, however, tends to focus on the influence of interest rates and income rather than on the payments mechanism. Interest elasticity of the demand for money has proved to be a more attractive subject of inquiry than the stability of bank float or the impact of the lockbox system on the speed of check collection. But since changes in payments technology and institutional arrangements seem to have played such an important role in the postwar rise in velocity, we shall review some of the technological factors which have contributed to the increase since World War II.

As velocity reflects shifts in attitudes toward money and liquidity, changes in payments habits, new cash management and banking techniques, and variations in the composition of payments flows, as well as other factors, the present study combines a scrutiny of the historical record with an examination of the underlying institutional and attitudinal factors. It brings up to date discussion of changes in payments patterns and banking techniques first examined nearly a decade ago.[3] The plan and scope of the present monograph differ, however, from those of its predecessor. Some of the descriptive material relating to institutional and technical factors has been condensed because adequate description is now readily available elsewhere. On the other hand, it has seemed desirable to draw from the large vol-

---

[3]*See George Garvy,* Deposit Velocity and Its Significance *(Federal Reserve Bank of New York, November 1959).*

ume of relevant published research, including econometric studies of the demand for money.

The velocity of money can be measured in a variety of ways. This study focuses on the two that are most widely used, namely, income velocity (V_y) and transactions velocity (V_t). Since much of current economic analysis and policy research centers on levels of aggregate output, it is not surprising that income velocity has come to play a more prominent role in academic literature than transactions velocity, which measures the intensity of use of the major component of the money supply, i.e., private demand deposits. Obviously, when analyzing financial-policy actions directed at influencing income and employment levels, income velocity is the more appropriate magnitude. Changes in flows of business and personal payments and in the money-transfer mechanism, on the other hand, can best be traced through the transactions approach. The two velocity concepts are clearly interrelated, and both ratios are significantly influenced by the degree to which, in the long run as well as cyclically, assets other than money acquire the attributes of "moneyness" and substitute for cash balances as liquidity reserves. At times, the two velocity measures move in opposite directions, for reasons to be discussed below.

The original version of this monograph concentrated on transactions velocity not only because the Federal Reserve Bank of New York pioneered as early as 1919 in developing this particular measure[4] but also because it was evident at the time that important changes in the technology of payments were taking place. These changes were given little recognition in academic discussion of the demand for money. They are, moreover, best studied in relation to patterns of aggregate payments rather than to the value of the final product. In the present completely revised version, the two measures of velocity are given equal attention. Since the analysis of velocity and that of the demand for cash balances are essentially alternative approaches to the same problem, some of our discussion is cast in terms of the demand for money.

One justification for paying the attention that we do to transactions velocity lies in the fact that a major part of the postwar rise in velocity reflects technological changes in our payments mechanism. Analysis of V_t emphasizes the dependence

---

[4]*See George Garvy,* The Development of Bank Debits and Clearings and Their Use in Economic Analysis *(Washington, D.C.: Board of Governors of the Federal Reserve System, 1952). A revised version was subsequently published under the title* Debits *and Clearings Statistics and Their Use (Board of Governors of the Federal Reserve System, 1959).*

of the demand for money on its technical efficiency in discharging payments obligations. Current discussion of an impending, though not imminent, shift from a check-ridden to a checkless society illustrates the extent to which the demand for money, and the velocity of its use, depend on specific technical arrangements.

Since the war years of excess liquidity, velocity has been increasing almost continuously in recessions and prosperity alike, though at differing rates. From a low of 1.97 in 1946, V_y increased to 4.59 in 1968; over the same years, V_t increased from 13.4 to 36.5. After rising substantially and almost continuously in the postwar decades, present levels are not much different from those attained in 1929, the previous peak. A number of important issues have been raised as a result of the postwar trend in velocity, aside from the perennial question of whether or not it is approaching some "velocity ceiling". First, there is the question of whether changes in velocity interfere with the effective execution of monetary policy, since such variations tend to offset changes in the money supply. A lively debate has been generated over the extent to which restrictive monetary measures aimed at reducing the rate of the money supply growth have been hampered or even negated by the more intensive use of money balances. Other policy-related questions have also been raised: Do shifts of funds between banks and nonbank financial institutions exert a destabilizing influence? To what extent is the behavior of velocity a function of interest rates? The list can be extended, but it is clear that an understanding of the reasons for short-term movements of velocity and for longer term trends is essential to the formulation of monetary policy. Academic debate of these and similar questions extends to attempts to rationalize postwar velocity changes in terms of changes in the demand for money. In doing so, the traditional Keynesian demand motives for holding cash balances have been subject to searching reappraisal, and the long-accepted view regarding the "uniqueness" of commercial banks among financial institutions has been questioned. A number of specific conclusions have been deduced from such reexamination, including the position taken by some economists that credit control should replace control of the money supply as the main objective of monetary policy.

Reasons for holding money balances are discussed in Chapter 2. Chapter 3 examines some of the factors influencing the main payments flows. Problems of measuring rates of money turnover are discussed in Chapter 4, and the statistical record is reviewed in Chapter 5. Chapter 6 deals with forces affecting velocity in the long run as well as over the business cycle. Implications of recent changes are assessed in the final chapter. In order not to burden the text, some of the technical detail has been relegated to two appendixes.

2. The Demand for Money

This study focuses on the narrow definition of money. Our preference for a definition of money limited to currency and demand deposits is rooted in the conviction that identification of money with the means of payment provides the most satisfactory analytical choice.

Of its various attributes, money plays a central role in the payments process. In a market economy, money is a carrier of options;[1] in fact, demand for money as a means of liquidity is a derivative of its role as the universal and absolute means of payment. The use of money as a liquidity reserve is predicated on its immunity to credit risk and its immediate exchangeability.

Of the several functions performed by money only a few can be dealt with quantitatively; among them, the demand for transactions purposes is paramount. Other reasons for holding cash, such as the "speculative" or "precautionary" motives frequently discussed, are more difficult to quantify and the related demands may be overlapping rather than additive.

Borrowers normally obtain credit in order to make payments rather than to add to balances. Borrowed money spent becomes part of the balance of the payee (business firms, consumers, governmental units, and others) until respent and/or used to retire bank (or other) debt. Even though extension of bank credit initially adds to the money supply, the aggregate demand function for cash balances by all spending units in the economy must not be confused with the demand for bank credit.

The reasons that individual economic groups wish to hold balances vary, but clearly the need to support an anticipated flow of payments is the most important.

---

[1] *In contrast to its role in centrally planned "command economies". See George Garvy, Money, Banking, and Credit in Eastern Europe (Federal Reserve Bank of New York, September 1966).*

The level of an average adequate balance depends, in addition to the level of expenditures, on the normal pattern of the flow of funds, the degree of probability of erratic peaks and troughs in these flows, and the ability of units to replenish their balances rapidly by borrowing or selling liquid assets. Thus, the management of a cash position could and does differ widely between industries and consumer groups and even within industries and consumer groups. Attitudes and practices are also diversified according to expectations, past experience, and available financial management techniques. A technical factor which influences the demand for cash balances is the compensatory balance requirement—well imbedded in the American banking scene—whereby loans are made and certain services performed by banks on condition that the customer maintain specified minimum or average balances. Another is the "day loan" which enables securities dealers to make during the day a large volume of payments from relatively small opening balances.[2]

In contemporary society, ownership of adequate cash balances is not an absolute prerequisite for acquiring goods and services or for discharging payments obligations. In fact, the relationship between holdings of money and current spending runs in both directions. The level of cash balances does not constitute a significant restraint on spending as long as economic units can replenish such balances by conversion of liquid assets or by borrowing. Furthermore, the relevant time horizon for spending units includes not only current but also future and past incomes. The accumulated stock of financial assets and the state of indebtedness—largely a result of past income and deficit spending history—are also relevant, not only as a determinant of the unit's willingness to spend, but also in establishing its access to credit. Another important fact is that for most economic units the flow of income in the immediate future is predictable within fairly narrow limits.

Greater assurance of access to money at times of need further weakens the link between cash balances and future spending. Informal or confirmed commercial bank credit lines for business firms and, more recently, overdraft facilities for households ("instant cash" and similar plans) tend to reduce the demand for cash in the bank. Issuance of demand claims is profitable to banks while it is onerous (in terms of opportunity costs) to the holder. However, to some extent a bank customer's ready access to additional money balances depends on the level of his balance, usually in relation to its use. Thus, the holding of balances for transactions

---

[2] See below, page 46.

15

purposes involves an element (compensating balances) that is also related to the ability of the holder to obtain additional cash resources in the future, either to support higher levels of spending (enlarging transactions balances) or to satisfy demands for asset diversification.

The demand for additional money to spend is not the same as the demand for money to hold. The demand for bank credit is, in the main, part of the total demand for credit—command over additional purchasing power; it is not the same as the demand for money balances as the means of liquidity *par excellence* which has been the object of intensive econometric research efforts during the recent decade. Obviously, as bank lending and investing expand in response to the demand for additional money to spend and aggregate spending rises, the need for balances to hold also increases. However, linkages between the demand for bank credit, as well as cash balances, to real output are complex. In particular, the extent to which the economy's demand for credit is satisfied by banks rather than other sources depends on a variety of factors which may or may not be relevant in determining the demand for money held in relation to the level of output and the demand for other liquidity instruments.

The relative position of the commercial banking system in the total flow of loanable funds reflects, in each given year, the extent to which the Federal Reserve System has provided reserves to permit commercial banks to accommodate the demand for credit beyond the amounts available as a result of the decisions of the various economic units to spend less than their current income. In war years, and when for other reasons the budget was in deficit, some or all of additional bank credit was created for the benefit of the United States Treasury. The importance of financial intermediaries as a source of credit has also fluctuated in relation to commercial banking and to direct lending. Changes in the degree of intermediation of credit through nonbank financial intermediaries are in part reflected in their demand for cash balances at banks, and at times in loan demand as well, since financial institutions maintain demand balances with commercial banks to meet operating needs for cash and, in particular, to provide holders of their liabilities with the means of payment as required.

While money is created predominantly through the lending and investing activities of banks, the extent to which expansion of bank credit will result in an addition to the money supply depends on the economy's willingness to retain money so created. These decisions, including those to convert part of the additional money supply into income-yielding time deposits, are made largely by units other than those which cause bank credit to expand in the first place, as loan-created balances

16

are disbursed to purchase goods and services, to pay taxes, or for other purposes. The outcome thus depends largely on decisions of units receiving payments, not of those originating loan demand.

The efficiency with which money is used by various spending units and economic sectors depends upon a number of factors, some of which are of an economic and others of a technical and institutional nature. Among the former, the availability and cost of credit is generally recognized as meriting special attention. Some of the latter have to do with differences in the timing of receipts and expenditures. Others can be traced to the space element in the payments process. When payment to a distant point is made by check, some time will elapse before the check is cleared and charged against the payer's account. The greater the proportion of payments made at distant points, the more will turnover rates be affected by delays in receiving check payments and in collecting the proceeds. The technology used in collecting checks and making the required bookkeeping entries has an important bearing on the efficiency with which the money supply is used and thus on the demand for cash balances, a subject more fully discussed in Chapter 6.

Autonomous changes in transactions levels usually generate accommodating shifts in the magnitude and composition of money demand between transactions balances and asset ("liquidity") balances which tend to be reflected by movements of velocity in the same direction as the changes in economic activity. It is, of course, not easy to ascertain to what extent a rise or fall in velocity is due to a change in composition of demand deposits, resulting from a shift in the purposes for which they are held, and to what extent a rise or fall in velocity is due to a more or less efficient use of deposits in making payments. In addition to purely technical factors, the demand for money responds to a variety of other factors, some of which are of a continuing nature, others arising from shifts in expectations and preferences—the latter frequently related to the whole constellation of interest rates, transactions costs, and other supply conditions which determine the opportunity cost of money in relation to other liquidity instruments.

DEFINITION OF MONEY

There is no general agreement on the proper definition of the money supply. Economists disagree as to which specific assets correspond most closely to the theoretical concept of money. The appropriate or preferable definition of financial assets constituting money differs from country to country, depending on numerous factors, such as institutional arrangements and the preferences of the individual

17

categories of transactors.[3] And, of course, these arrangements and preferences are not stable over time.

An important consideration concerns whether or not and which time deposits should be included.[4] Many monetary analysts exclude savings and other time deposits from the money supply on the grounds that, while they are (in contrast to other money substitutes) a commercial bank liability, they must be converted into checkbook or folding money before they can be spent. Even though time deposits cannot perform the payments function of money, they can and do, in common with other money substitutes, satisfy in varying degrees the liquidity needs of at least certain sectors of the economy. Commercial bank savings deposits, for instance, compete with savings and loan shares as an outlet for financial savings of households, while negotiable certificates of deposit (CD's) issued by commercial banks compete with other money market instruments as a means of fulfilling the liquidity needs of corporations.

The question of the degree of "moneyness" of savings and time deposits[5] has been subject to a lively debate, especially since the publication of the important studies by Gurley-Shaw and Friedman-Schwartz.[6] Various statistical investigations suggest

---

[3]*Monetary authorities of various countries, no less than economists, have tried to come to grips with this problem when publishing monetary statistics. See, for instance, the* Monetary Survey *of the* International Monetary Fund. *Once-and-for-all decisions are difficult to make. Thus, particularly since the late 1950's, the rising velocity of circulation of certain savings balances, evidencing their greater use in making payments, has caused the Netherlands Bank to classify certain types of savings balances as "near moneys".*

[4]*Proponents of the view that changes in the money supply are the direct cause of change in the level of economic activity do not agree on the proper definition of the money supply. Milton Friedman's empirical tests are based on a definition which includes time deposits of commercial banks, while Leonall C. Andersen and his associates at the Federal Reserve Bank of St. Louis prefer the conventional narrow concept.*

[5]*According to the call report of June 1968, 62 percent of all time deposits in commercial banks are personal savings deposits; the remainder are business, government, foreign, or bank time deposits.*
Inquiries conducted by the Federal Reserve System in the midthirties, together with data currently collected by the American Bankers Association and the Federal Reserve Bank of Chicago, indicate that withdrawals from savings accounts during a given year amount to about half of the average balance. In other words, savings deposits turn over about once every two years. This ratio has been quite stable from year to year (except in 1966 when it rose significantly) and appears to be little influenced by changes in business activity. For a detailed discussion, see George Garvy, "The Velocity of Time Deposits", Journal of the American Statistical Association *(June 1953). For a more recent discussion, see "Slowing in Savings Deposit Growth and Turnover",* Business Conditions *(Federal Reserve Bank of Chicago, June 1964) and "The Rise in CD's at District Banks", ibid. (October 1965).*

[6]*John G. Gurley and Edward S. Shaw,* Money in a Theory of Finance *(Washington, D.C., 1960) and Milton Friedman and Anna J. Schwartz,* A Monetary History of the United States, 1867-1960 *(Princeton, New Jersey, 1963). See also David M. Jones,* The Demand for Money: A Review of the Empirical Literature *(Federal Reserve Bank of New York, 1965, mimeographed), briefly summarized in the* Federal Reserve Bulletin *(February 1966), pages 164-65.*

that marginal changes in the flow of income are related to marginal changes in the stock of savings deposits as well as to changes in the stock of money, narrowly defined. One investigator, using data for the period 1947-66, found that the stock of savings deposits, variously defined, possessed some significant degrees of moneyness which decreased as the concept of savings deposits gradually broadened to include savings deposits at mutual savings banks, postal savings deposits, and ultimately savings and loan shares along with time deposits at commercial banks.[7] Tests along these or similar lines merely indicate that, in some periods at least, marginal changes of income are correlated in varying degrees with changes in the stock of selected financial assets. They do not establish (or disprove) the moneyness of time deposits or other near moneys. Instead they merely suggest that changes in financial assets are among the factors which, in addition to money, influence the level of economic activity. And, to use Professor B. Pesek's words, "to test, first, all sorts of conglomerates of liquid assets and only subsequently give the name 'money' to one that correlates best makes monetary theory vacuous since it is not subject to contradiction; surely a modern computer will always come up with some conglomerate that correlates well with income".[8]

The interaction of a rising opportunity cost of money and of advances in cash-saving technology has induced consumers, no less than other major categories of economic units, to rely on money substitutes for meeting a large part of their liquidity needs, converting such claims into money as needed. For all practical purposes, savings deposits at mutual savings banks and savings and loan shares are regarded by their owners as adequate substitutes for commercial bank savings deposits. Thus, the proper dividing line is not between total commercial bank deposits and other money substitutes, but between demand deposits and all other

[7]G. S. Laumas, "The Degree of Moneyness of Savings Deposits", American Economic Review, (June 1968), pages 501-3. In fact, by including all commercial bank time deposits, this analysis is not limited to savings deposits, but also includes negotiable certificates of deposit and other time deposits held by corporations and others. See also T. H. Lee, "Substitutability of Nonbank Intermediary Liabilities for Money: The Empirical Evidence", Journal of Finance (September 1966), pages 441-57.
Other investigators, who limited their analysis to commercial bank time deposits, arrived at similar conclusions (and a virtually identical estimate of moneyness) for the eleven years (1929-39) preceding World War II and for the years following it, but found that such deposits possessed a negative degree of moneyness for other periods. R. H. Timberlake and J. Forton, "Time Deposits in the Definition of Money", American Economic Review (March 1967), pages 190-94.

[8]The Journal of Finance (December 1968), page 904.

deposit claims (including savings and loan shares).[9] How households choose to distribute their assets among the various forms of liquidity (money, savings deposits, or in other ways) depends upon a number of considerations, including relative rates of return, transactions costs, safety, and convenience. Instead of searching for a "broad" definition of money that would be consistently valid over a fairly protracted period of time—say one generation—it would appear preferable to focus our investigation on the narrower definition of money and to explore how changes in asset preferences have influenced changes in its velocity.

MONEY SUBSTITUTES

Money is different from other financial assets because it does not yield any explicit income.[10] Between money and largely illiquid assets, such as pension rights, stands an array of financial claims, each unique in one or more respects and each at the same time competing for inclusion in portfolios of liquid assets. The degree of liquidity of money substitutes (also referred to as "near money") is usually defined in terms of convertibility into money, the liquidity instrument *par excellence*.

Most but not all money substitutes are liabilities of financial intermediaries: short-term Government securities and commercial paper issued by industrial corporations, for example, are not. On the other hand, of the two nondepository financial intermediaries with the largest volume of assets—life insurance companies and personal trust funds, including pension funds—only the first provides a limited degree of liquidity to individuals (through policy loans); neither supplies any liquidity instruments that can be used as money substitutes.

While money substitutes do not possess liquidity to the same extent as money, they do offer the benefit of an interest return. Still more important, this return comes with no great sacrifice of liquidity, for claims against thrift institutions and money market instruments are readily convertible into cash at the option of the

---

[9]*See Michael J. Hamburger, "Household Demand for Financial Assets",* Econometrica *(January 1968). See, in particular, his conclusion on page 105 where references are given to several studies confirming as well as disagreeing with this conclusion. This article also contains an extensive bibliography on the demand for money. See also George G. Kaufman, "More on an Empirical Definition of Money",* American Economic Review *(March 1969).*

[10]*This is not a universal characteristic of money. The prohibition against payment of interest on demand deposits did not exist in the United States prior to 1933, and interest is paid on sight deposits in some foreign countries.*

holder. Money market instruments, other than those issued by the Federal Govern-ment, are subject to some degree of credit risk. However, the short-term nature of the claims and the high financial standing of their issuers reduce loss expectations to a minimum.

Over the postwar period, money substitutes have come to comprise a steadily increasing proportion of liquid assets portfolios (see Chart 1), in part as a result of the upward trend of interest rates. As a consequence, especially since the early fifties, economic units have been adjusting their liquidity reserves to include a greater share of interest-bearing claims and a smaller share of currency and

Chart 1. **MONEY AS A PERCENTAGE OF TOTAL LIQUID ASSET HOLDINGS 1953-68**

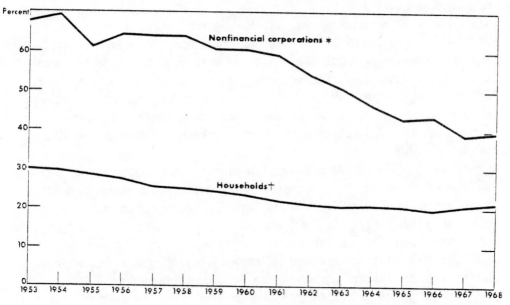

* In addition to money, the liquid assets held by nonfinancial corporations include time deposits, short-term United States Government securities, and commercial paper.

† In addition to demand deposits and currency (i.e., money), liquid assets held by the household sector include time and savings deposits at commercial banks and savings institutions, short-term United States Government securities, and savings bonds.

Source: Board of Governors of the Federal Reserve System, *Federal Reserve Bulletin*, Flow of Funds Accounts.

demand deposits. While the demand for transactions purposes may be presumed to be less interest elastic than that for asset-holding purposes, significant increases in interest rates tend to lead to reassessment of minimum transactions balance needs.

In the last two decades, numerous attempts have been made to resolve the issue by econometric analysis of the behavior of various types of financial assets in order to determine which of them come closest to money, narrowly defined. Various authors either have widened the definition of money on the basis of their interpretation of the results of their inquiries or have suggested alternatively that certain groups of assets be considered as money substitutes. Of course, there is no more agreement as to the empirical scope and theoretical interpretation of such categories than there is on the proper definition of money. The general nature of the process which, since the revival of monetary policy in the early 1950's, has led to a massive shift of funds from demand deposits into money substitutes is, however, fairly simple to describe.

Business firms, households, state and local governments, and eleemosynary institutions, as well as foreign holders of dollar balances, can reduce the opportunity cost of holding adequate cash balances by investing in money market instruments that are readily convertible into cash and which involve a minimum of risk. Since the fifties, there has been a proliferation of tailor-made market instruments and arrangements to meet various corporate needs (as well as similar requirements of other large depositors, such as municipal governments) and liberalization of time contracts available to individuals. As shifts from cash into income-yielding liquidity instruments and back into cash involve certain transactions costs, it became unprofitable in periods of very low money market rates, which characterized the thirties and the subsequent World War II period, to economize on cash balances. The situation changed again in 1951, when rates began to rise after the "Accord" and as various borrowers and intermediaries in the money market began to develop instruments to meet the specific needs of various groups of demanders for money substitutes. In recent years, a practice has developed where banks agree to "borrow" from corporate and other large depositors all demand balances above a certain agreed minimum amount. Since such borrowing—even for one day—is not prohibited so long as it is secured, redundant balances are absorbed by the bank and the customer's balance is kept at a workable minimum, showing a higher velocity than would otherwise be the case.

Periods of high interest rates usually coincide with periods of active and rising business. In such periods, there is an opportunity to make additional cash outlays

22

on goods and services without correspondingly adding to cash balances, and it becomes more profitable to exchange money for other financial claims. As a result, measured turnover rates increase. Parallel, but opposite, reasoning suggests that money turnover rates decline in periods of low interest rates. It is quite obvious that shifts in the composition of portfolios of various holder groups between money and all other liquid assets combined affect cyclical and, more importantly, secular velocity.

THE ROLE OF FINANCIAL MARKETS

Liquidity is synonymous with salability or shiftability, which, in turn, requires the existence of efficient financial markets.[11]

The development of the money market, in which the various categories of financial intermediaries participate (although to varying degrees), along with the growth of large manufacturing and other corporations, has increased the moneyness of those financial instruments and arrangements that have come to compete with demand deposits as a means of liquidity. Essential elements in the creation of this market have been, first, the existence of a large number of participants, with seasonally varying needs and different degrees of sensitivity to cyclical influences and, second, the availability of a wide range of instruments of differing maturities and legal characteristics suited to the varied requirements of lenders and borrowers. In this market, liquidity is provided through shiftability and partly because of the variety of needs of the participants, as some investors are always willing to trade maturity for income. This shiftability, in turn, depends to a large extent on the efficiency of dealers, brokers, and other intermediaries who establish markets, seek out investable funds, and periodically develop new techniques, such as repurchase agreements on Government securities. It is the development of the money market, with the perfection of its operating techniques, and the participation of the banking system in this market that have been instrumental in narrowing the gap between money and money substitutes.

While individual units can easily convert money market assets in the market, all

---

[11]In recent decades several advanced countries have experienced a very rapid growth of financial intermediaries, in some cases paired with a spectacular growth of public debt, without showing a parallel substitution of near moneys for money. One reason is that they did not succeed in developing a sufficiently broad money market with a proper range of instruments and techniques.

economic units combined can "shift into cash" only to the extent that banks are able and willing to acquire such assets on balance. Thus, the ease of access to additional money, through borrowing or conversion of assets, is influenced by current and prospective monetary policy.

SYNCHRONIZATION OF RECEIPTS AND EXPENDITURES

Money as a means of payment is essential for completing most, if not all, transactions arising in a modern economy. The flow of goods through the various stages of production and distribution involves payments to the various agents of production, such as labor and capital. Normally, whenever the ownership of either intermediate or final products passes from one economic unit to another, additional debits to the account of one unit or more (when brokers or agencies are involved) arise. As the flow of revenues is not perfectly matched to the flow of payments, business units hold cash balances to meet payments when they fall due. The amount of cash held in relation to the volume of payments depends, in part, on the opportunity cost of holding money as well as on purely technical factors, such as the frequency of receipts (which itself depends on billing practices and the characteristic seasonal pattern of sales in each given industry) and the schedule of disbursements (in which the frequency of wage and salary payments and of purchases of raw materials are among the more important influences). This holds true for all categories of transactions—business, consumers, nonprofit institutions, and units at all levels of government.

Mathematical models have been developed to show that the need for cash balances declines with improvements in synchronization of the flow of personal and business payments to receipts; the shorter the pay period, the smaller the balance which the average consumer will have to hold in relation to expenditures.[12] The various relevant factors are usually discussed in textbooks under such headings as "income periods", "overlapping of payments", or "time intervals" between interfirm payments.[13]

---

[12]*Suppose a worker is paid every four weeks and spends his entire income evenly over that period. With a paycheck of $400, he will keep an average cash balance of $200 and the annual turnover rate is 26 times the average cash balance. But assume instead that he receives a weekly paycheck: his average cash balance now is $50, while the rate of turnover increases to 104.*

[13]*See, in particular, Irving Fisher,* Purchasing Power of Money *(New York, 1911); J. W. Angell, "The Components of the Circular Velocity of Money",* The Quarterly Journal of Economics *(February 1937), and H. S. Ellis, "Some Fundamentals in the Theory of Velocity", ibid., May 1938.*

Changes in typical payment periods occur from time to time, particularly in the business sphere. Business firms may shift to new payments or billing procedures (such as cycle billing) with the specific purpose of improving the synchronization of their cash flows and reducing transactions balances besides spreading out the work load. Corporate treasurers of large firms with diversified products are usually better able to anticipate and synchronize payments flows than independent units linked by market relationships, with all the attendant uncertainties and needs for protective margins. The fewer the number of independent business units involved as a product moves through the various stages of production and distribution, the fewer the number of potential gaps between receipts and expenditures. The precise way in which growing integration in production and distribution, particularly through corporate mergers, reduces the need for transactions balances depends on how payments between formerly separate establishments are handled after they are combined.

The problem of synchronization is not limited to production and distribution of current output. It is pertinent also to trading in financial assets, since not all sales of financial assets are immediately matched by purchases. Transactions in financial assets, being determined by such considerations as the relative yield patterns of various types of securities and the liquidity needs of business firms and individuals, lack the regularity of wage, rent, tax, dividend, and other payments which flow from the process of producing and distributing current output. As a result, the level of cash balances arising from, or held in connection with, trading in financial markets varies with business conditions, interest rates, and other factors. In particular, when investors shift from securities (and other financial assets) into cash, the velocity of cash balances is reduced.

FACTORS TENDING TO REDUCE THE DEMAND FOR TRANSACTIONS MONEY

Even though money is first of all a means of payment, not all income-producing or asset transactions require its use. Numerous institutional arrangements have been developed to minimize the amount of cash used in trading financial assets. Payments also can be offset or obviated, reducing the demand for cash balances, as discussed in more detail in Chapter 6. The use of book credit and the offsetting of interbusiness payments tend to reduce cash needs as well, but it is uncertain whether the relative importance of industries in which interbusiness financing and/or the use of book credit are significant has increased or decreased over the years.

Payments may also be made without the use of money, depending on the convenience to the payer and the willingness of the payee to accept (or even to require) substitutes as well as on habits and facilities offered. For instance, a not inconsiderable volume of goods and services is paid for by endorsing checks received. Credit instruments circulating as money substitutes are limited now almost entirely to drafts, but in earlier periods, and even currently in some foreign countries, trade bills, acceptances, and similar instruments have to be considered as substitutes for money. Government securities issued for the specific purpose of being accepted in lieu of cash (tax anticipation bills) and Treasury securities acceptable in payment of estate taxes are other examples of payments not requiring cash.

Finally, various means of payment for special purposes have been developed in exchange for money. They include traveler's checks, money orders, and even tokens, such as those used by public transportation systems.[14] Conversion of universal money into special payments instruments increases income velocity by reducing average money balances held and also affects transactions velocity. It is unlikely that the proportion of payments made without the use of money is subject to significant short-run fluctuations (nor is it particularly sensitive to changes in monetary policy), but it may need to be considered in long-run comparisons.

Important changes in the demand for money stem from the ability of various categories of holders to increase the efficiency of transactions balances. Specific policies to achieve such economies are discussed in Chapter 6. More efficient use of deposit balances is reflected in increased transactions velocity, unless offset by an increase of balances held for liquidity purposes or for other reasons not directly related to the volume of current check payments.

Greater efficiency in the use of deposit balances has clearly been one of the main influences behind the post-World War II rise in the income velocity of money. Another important influence has been the growing tendency for liquidity and other reserves and temporarily redundant funds to be invested in money market instruments; fewer and fewer households are now content to let savings accumulate in nonearning demand deposits.

---

[14]*For example, the demand for dimes dropped abruptly in New York when subway fares went up and tokens were substituted for dimes.*

In older literature, balances not needed for transactions purposes were sometimes bracketed as "idle" or "excess" balances. The distinction between "active" and "idle" balances is, however, essentially an expository device. Demand deposit accounts that are virtually dormant for prolonged periods of time (or that are occasionally increased but not drawn against) are exceptions; nearly all accounts show some degree of activity. In effect, idle balances are an abstraction referring to amounts in excess of those normally required to meet a given flow of payments.[15] For each business firm, individual, or other spending unit, the amount of idle balances depends on a number of factors, in addition to interest rates, such as liquidity needs arising from the nature of the account owner's business and his plans for the future, the geographic and time patterns of payments, and the requirements of the banks as to minimum or compensating balances. These factors may be subject to long-run as well as cyclical influences. For example, those who hold cash for speculative purposes may change their expectations regarding prices of goods and/or services as well as yields on securities, and they may decide to use the balances they have built up to acquire other goods, services, or securities as the favorable situations which they have anticipated begin to materialize.

This process, referred to as "activation of idle balances", is best looked upon as a reshuffling of liquid-asset holdings when interest rates rise. As the volume of payments expands with business activity, some existing balances are found to be ample enough to support additional transactions and their turnover rates accordingly increase. Other accounts which are close to minimum needs have to be built up by borrowing or by converting liquid assets into cash; their rates of turnover may not change much, as balances and transactions rise more or less in step, but the growth of such balances will enlarge the share of more active accounts in total demand deposits. Statistical data recording rising turnover velocity in periods when the pace of economic activity accelerates reflect additional debits generated by various cash management activities as well as a cyclical reduction of the share of idle money in the total money supply.

---

[15]For a pioneering study of "excess cash" estimated by applying minimum cash-sales ratios achieved in 1929, see Avram Kisselgoff, "Liquidity Preference of Large Manufacturing Corporations", Econometrica (October 1945), pages 334-44.

It is usually assumed that the size of the average cash balance held by each economic unit is regulated by its transactions and liquidity requirements. In fact, however, balances also serve to compensate banks for the services they perform, including the handling of payments and the providing of credit facilities. Indeed, a substantial part of banking services, in particular the maintaining of regular business accounts, is paid for in the United States by appropriate compensating balances. Such balances are a large proportion of total demand deposits, although the total amount of deposits held as compensatory balances is not known.[16] This practice is peculiar to American banking, Canada being the only other country in which compensating balances are used. Furthermore, the amount of compensating balances lodged with the commercial banking system and the changes in this amount caused by cyclical or other influences are significant factors in explaining the behavior of velocity.

Individuals as well as businesses usually have, within certain limits, an option either to pay a service charge for the handling of their accounts or to compensate their banks indirectly by maintaining balances on which the banks can earn an income equivalent to the service charge.[17] The laws often make it advantageous for individuals to pay for banking services through compensating balances. The depositor forgoes income on the balance maintained, but in many cases he would have had to invest a larger amount in order to earn enough income after taxes to pay bank charges.

Corporations pay service charges for routine bank services (such as account activity, preparation of payrolls, wire transfer of funds, credit inquiries, etc.) only in exceptional cases, for instance, when services are used intermittently or when the bank's deposit requirements are judged by the corporation to be excessive.

---

[16]*See also Jack M. Guttentag and Richard G. Davis, "Compensating Balances", Monthly Review (Federal Reserve Bank of New York, December 1961), pages 205-10. See also Thomas Mayer and Ira O. Scott, Jr., "Compensatory Balances: A Suggested Interpretation", The National Banking Review (December 1963), pages 157-66, which cites the result of a survey conducted by them suggesting that banks, in fact, pay an imputed interest on compensating balances and that most banks administer the compensating balance requirements in a flexible manner, and W. E. Gibson, "Compensating Balance Requirements", The National Banking Review (March 1965). For a recent sample survey, see H. G. Hamel and F. J. Walsh, Jr., Commercial Banking Arrangements, Managing the Financial Function, No. 3 (New York: National Industrial Conference Board, 1968).*

[17]*The United States Government also compensates commercial banks for certain services by keeping appropriate balances; see H. J. Cooke, "Managing the Treasury's Cash Balances", in The Treasury and the Money Market (Federal Reserve Bank of New York, May 1954) pages 7-11.*

Those bank services to business firms that normally give rise to the payment of explicit service charges are corporate trust services (e.g., the issuance of dividend checks and stock certificate transfers). In recent years, the institution by banks of various "bookkeeping"-type services has led to an increase in the amount of bank charges.

Although the idea of service charges began to take root before the turn of the century, by 1929 (when banks still paid interest on demand deposit accounts) only a little more than one third of all banks had adopted the practice of charging for services rendered. The depression, but also the discussion of banking codes under the National Recovery Administration, boosted the movement toward the application of service charges. Subsequently, account analysis became almost general practice, and payment for banking services by maintaining adequate balances was encouraged.[18] In general, since World War II, and particularly in recent years, there has been a tendency to place the "pricing" of banking services on the same basis as in nonbanking businesses.[19] Charges levied for various types of services, and the rate used to compute earnings credit, vary considerably among banks. Banks periodically analyze the activity of business and other large accounts in order to determine their profitability. Activity charges are computed through a fairly standardized analysis based on the principle that earnings credit allowed on average (or minimum) balances, after deduction for applicable legal reserves, should be equal to the actual cost incurred plus a fair profit margin. Most banks compute earnings credit on the basis of collected balances, but others compute them on ledger balances.

Corporate treasurers usually review independently the account analyses made by their banks. In considering the proper level of compensating balances, they may allow for perhaps an even wider range of services than those considered by the banks by taking into account various intangible services performed by banks. In addition to the routine banking services, services rendered to the customer's employees, such as assisting transferred employees in locating and financing homes,

---

[18]The American Bankers Association issued in 1935 its first Manual for Determining Per Item Costs, followed in 1939 by Uniform Account Analysis.

[19]See James P. Furness and Paul S. Nadler, "Should Banks Reprice Corporate Services?" in Harvard Business Review (May-June 1966). Whether and how profitable the compensating balance requirement is for the commercial banks is a matter of debate. See Richard G. Davis and Jack M. Guttentag, "Balances Requirements and Deposit Competition", The Journal of Political Economy (December 1963) and William G. DeWald, "The Economics of Compensating Balances", Iowa Business Review (July 1965), and the literature quoted therein.

may also be given recognition. Considerations relating to community goodwill or the maintenance of long-established banking connections may also play a role. Some corporations maintain as a matter of policy a certain minimum balance with each bank in their network of local depositories.[20]

In general, compensating balances are determined as a percentage—usually 15 percent to 20 percent—of the amount of borrowing outstanding, or about 10 percent to 20 percent of credit lines granted. Normally, neither consumer nor mortgage loans involve commensurate balances, nor do most types of financial loans such as those to brokers. The share of commensurate balances in the total deposits of a given bank will depend on the composition of its loan portfolio. This is significant when comparing turnover ratios among individual banks or localities and where assessing long-run changes in transactions velocity in the light of changes in the composition of assets of the banking system as a whole.

The total amount of compensating balances maintained is determined by the primary functions which they are intended to perform, namely, to compensate banks for costs incurred in rendering a wide range of services and to assure adequate access to credit. Yet, at the same time, such balances may satisfy part or all of the liquidity requirements of their owners. Since compensating balances are normally based on average rather than on minimum balances, they can be drawn down temporarily to meet unexpected drains on funds, usually at the cost of incurring service charges, and rebuilt when the customer is "in funds". Many business customers rightly consider compensating balances as part of their liquidity reserves.

Banks, in particular large institutions, also ordinarily require or expect their customers to maintain appropriate balances in return for the extension of credit lines.[21] Such balances are also referred to as compensating balances, although occa-

[20]*See George Katona,* Business Looks at Banks *(Ann Arbor, Michigan: 1957), Chapter 6. Also J. E. Walter, "Liquidity and Corporate Spending",* Journal of Finance *(December 1953), pages 369-87.*

[21]*According to a recent sample survey, roughly two fifths of commercial banks with total deposits of less than $20 million require compensating balances, while for larger banks, with deposits of $150 million and over, the percentage rose to nearly 100. Even in the case of relatively small banks (between $20 million and $50 million), the percentage is about 85. The use of compensating balance requirements has become increasingly more widespread since the emergence of greater rate fluctuations after the "Accord" of 1951. Only about half of all commercial banks requiring compensating balances in 1964 did so before 1951, when the practice was limited mostly to larger banks. Thus, 80 percent of the banks with over $1 billion in deposits who required compensating balances in 1964 did so before 1951, but only 15 percent of the banks with deposits of under $20 million. Nevins D. Baxter and Harold T. Shapiro, "Compensating Balance Requirements: The Result of a Survey",* Journal of Finance *(September 1964). See also "Credit Lines and Minimum Balance Requirements",* Federal Reserve Bulletin *(June 1956), pages 573-79 for data based on the October 1955 survey of*

sionally "commensurate" or "supporting" balances is used to distinguish them from balances required to compensate banks for checking and similar services. Commensurate balances apply with varying frequency to almost all types of business borrowers, and are determined by the category and size of the customer. Some banks require commensurate balances only from certain categories of borrowers, such as finance companies.

Frequently, corporations which do not establish formal credit lines maintain sufficiently large balances with their principal banks in order to facilitate access to credit in the case of urgent need. Indeed, most banks that have no formal minimum balance requirements would take a customer's usual deposit balance into account when providing loan accommodation and in setting the interest rate on a loan. Banks look at commensurate balances as an important aspect of overall bank-customer relationships. Compensating balances are sensitive to interest rates but only to a limited extent. The earnings credit, on the basis of which the size of balances required to compensate for account activity is computed, moves with the general level of interest rates, but rates used for computing earnings credit are adjusted only when major changes in interest levels take place, and even then with a lag.[22] Commensurate balances to support borrowing and related goodwill balances are, on the whole, also rather insensitive to fluctuations in interest rates. Nevertheless, under the pressure of high or rising interest rates, some depositors maintaining a large number of accounts will tend to eliminate certain low-activity and duplicating accounts. On the other hand, bankers will place more emphasis on balances when loan demand is strong and use commensurate balances as a credit-rationing device.

The lodgment in the deposit structure of a large volume of compensating balances therefore has the effect of dampening cyclical swings in velocity. Their aggregate volume tends to be related to account activity and loan volume; and any increase in account activity and loans granted or committed calls for an increase in compensating balances. Compensating balance requirements may be raised, their

[21](continued from page 30):

commercial and industrial loans at member banks, and D. P. Jacobs, "Sources and Costs of Funds of Large Sales Finance Companies", Consumer Instalment Credit, Part II, Vol. 1 (Washington, D.C.: Board of Governors of the Federal Reserve System, 1957), pages 341-52.

[22]If, in a period of expansion, reserve requirements are raised, higher earnings credit may be offset, in part or entirely, since required reserves are deducted from compensating balances on which the earnings credit is based.

use may be extended to a greater number of borrowers, and perhaps most important the requirements are definitely more vigorously enforced. To the extent commensurate balances come to exceed the balances that corporations would voluntarily keep, the effective yield on loans is increased. At the same time, the fact that the total volume of usable bank credit (demand deposits) is reduced acts as a brake on velocity: the greater the amount of compensating balances held for various purposes in total demand deposits, the smaller is the computed velocity. The relationship between compensating balances and economic activity and the level of interest rates is sufficiently complex to deserve specific recognition in econometric studies of the "demand for money", especially when analysis is extended to the twenties; unfortunately, such studies have generally disregarded this relationship.[23]

MODELS OF DEMAND FOR MONEY

Availability of a variety of pertinent data on a current basis has encouraged construction of increasingly complex econometric models of the demand for money. The relationship of money to spending can be analyzed in numerous ways. Simple models usually take as a starting point the transactions demand for money, and they demonstrate how the level of returns available on near moneys tends to be associated with efforts to economize on cash balances.

Transactions balances are not reported separately. Since direct and independent measurements of either the aggregate payments flow or the demand for financial assets are also not available, empirical studies of the demand for money relate transactions demand to some index of current economic activity. Among these, gross national product (GNP) in current dollars figures predominantly because of its comprehensiveness. The time profile of the various velocity series has been explained in terms of the interaction of variables of a cyclical kind (e.g., interest rates) or of a long-run nature (such as rising average income or accumulation of financial assets). Others have sought explanations in structural changes in the economy or in payments streams (see below page 58).

The simple receipt-and-disbursement model, which concludes that the trans-

---

[23]*Prior to 1933 commercial banks generally paid interest on demand deposits, and holding of compensating balances in the current sense was not widespread. This is one of the major reasons why in the fifties the transactions velocity of demand deposits was considerably lower than in the twenties, in spite of the great progress that had been made in collecting and managing funds by large holders of demand balances.*

actions balance will average half of the total flow (assuming that cash is available at the beginning of the period and that payments have a fair degree of regularity), can be made more realistic by allowing for investment of part of the balance in income-earning assets and resorting to short-term borrowing to meet scheduled disbursements during the latter part of the period. Such a model can be made even more realistic by explicitly introducing the cost of engaging in asset-switching operations and the cost of negotiating loans. Tested against empirical data for the period 1947 to 1965, one such model yields significant results which show that the average transactions balances held in the form of cash are related positively to the cost of borrowed funds and negatively to the return on long-term investments.[24] Demand-for-money models can be, and have been, made more complex by introducing the diversification demand for money. The demand for money as a financial asset is not related importantly to the current level of economic activity. The volume of financial assets existing at any given time is the cumulative result of experience over a period of years, and thus diversification demand for money is not directly related to current product or income alone. Neither is it necessary to assume that lags involved in the demand for money in relation to the various determining factors are stable over time or identical for all sectors.

Numerous empirical studies have been undertaken to clarify the question of whether the demand for money is primarily a function of money's unique characteristic as a universal means of payment (and thus related to some variant of income) or a function of wealth as its owners attempt to diversify holdings (thus making portfolio diversification an important factor of demand), or both. Virtually all such studies have found money balances to be responsive to money rates, but there is little agreement on whether the cost of bank borrowing or rates on assets competing with money and whether short- or long-term rates are relevant. Since business expansions are normally accompanied by rising interest rates, it is not surprising that many researchers have found in fluctuations of interest rates a ready explanation for the cyclical behavior of rates of money turnover.[25] Though statistically significant relationships between interest rates and either of the two measures

---

[24]E. L. Whalen, "An Extension of the Baumol-Tobin Approach to the Transactions Demand for Cash", Journal of Finance (March 1968).

[25]Since the publication of the frequently quoted article by Henry A. Latané, "Cash Balances and the Interest Rate: A Pragmatic Approach", Review of Economics and Statistics (November 1954), pages 456-60, the literature on this subject has grown extensively. Widening the concept of money usually results in reducing interest elasticity.

of velocity are readily established, it is not possible to determine precisely to what extent fluctuations in velocity are caused directly and uniquely by changes in the attractiveness of yields available on money market instruments (or thrift deposits).[26]

Demand-for-money models can be complex. They may, for instance, allow for a "learning process" with regard to the demand for money substitutes. They can recognize the fact that costs incurred in establishing a money-management function within a corporate structure are not simply written off when rates drop below a certain level. Money market participation is continued in such periods in order, among other things, to preserve access to the market at times when participation in it would prove profitable. This "institutionalization" of response patterns, operating independently of initial economic stimuli, has not as yet been adequately explored.

Demand-for-money models as a rule make a number of simplifying explicit or implicit assumptions, many of which are questionable, such as the assumptions that cash holdings are proportional to outlays and that lags are constant over time. The general difficulty with all these models is the assumption that motivation can be dealt with on a universal basis, using national (aggregate) series for empirical verification, while in fact relevant factors underlying the demand for money differ significantly among major economic segments and spender categories.[27] The demand function for money must be differentiated for the various categories of holders of cash balances. Patterns of financial asset holdings vary widely. Cash inventory demand of individuals differs from that of business.

Much of the underlying theoretical literature is cast in terms of the demand of individuals for money balances. In fact, business firms are the largest single holder group, and their cash balances are more likely to be subject to cyclical and long-

---

[26]*For a theoretical model of cyclical variations in velocity that does not consider interest rates at all, see Milton Friedman, The Demand for Money: Some Theoretical and Empirical Results, Occasional Paper 68 (New York: National Bureau of Economic Research, 1959). Karl Brunner and Allan H. Meltzer—"Economies of Scale in Cash Balances Reconsidered", The Quarterly Journal of Economics (August 1967), pages 422-36—deny that economies of scale contradict the quantity theory of money and question the claim that such economies in the demand of business firms for money are implicit in the Baumol and Tobin models.*

[27]*For one of the few exceptions, see M. J. Hamburger, "The Demand for Money by Households, Money Substitutes, and Monetary Policy", The Journal of Political Economy (December 1966).*
Unfortunately, data on money holdings by the main economic sectors are not available, and even the limited data on deposit ownership for 1943 to 1961 and estimates prepared in connection with the flow of funds are based on a set of broad assumptions, usually held unvaried over long periods of time, thus failing to reflect many important structural and institutional changes as well as changes in processes and procedures.

run changes than those held by consumers. Thus, while household wealth may be a factor in the diversification of money, it is not pertinent for cash holdings of corporations which are estimated to hold half of the money supply. Rates on negotiable CD's have been relevant since 1961 in determining corporate demand for cash, but they are significant for only a comparatively small group of wealthy individuals. Rates available on savings and loan shares are probably more important for individuals as a factor in determining the attractiveness of demand as well as of time deposits at commercial banks, but are largely irrelevant for corporations which cannot hold such shares.

Emphasis on interest rates and/or on the income or wealth variable (e.g., GNP, Friedman's "permanent income") has the limitations inherent in all types of analysis searching for a universally valid "first cause". Yet, to explain money demand in the middle sixties, for instance, as responding in an unvarying way to interest rate movements is wholly to ignore the facts that liquidity management has become an integral part of the overall financial management function and that economizing on balances has become a structuralized part of portfolio management. Looked at from the corporate treasurer's point of view, money has fallen in stature from liquidity *par excellence* to one of several liquidity instruments (that is, as a liquid asset having a number of substitutes), to a costly inventory, the amount of which should be reduced at every opportunity.

Before proceeding further, we should emphasize that the available statistical data on the money supply, including its short-term changes and ownership by principal economic sectors, are quite deficient, and the prospects for remedying them in the near future are dim. Indeed, empirical studies of the demand for money are beset by a variety of theoretical and technical problems. One important difficulty is that adequate empirical data has become more readily available only since the end of World War II, a period of rapidly rising income and mild cyclical fluctuations in the United States and elsewhere. As a result, any time series is dominated by a strong upward trend; but the problem of the high degree of correlation between all relevant series extends to their similar response to cyclical influences as well. Much of the published research related to the use of money, whether approached in terms of demand or velocity, is handicapped by these limitations. One conclusion emerges clearly from the historical record whatever the shortcomings of the underlying statistical series: the velocity of money is not constant over time, and policy recommendations based on such an assumption disregard an essential aspect of economic and monetary processes. We shall return to this issue in Chapter 7. In the meantime, it will be useful to keep in mind that changes in velocity may

35

be due to any combination of the following factors:

(1) structure of payments flows, including financial flows,
(2) opportunity cost of money in relation to the yield of substitutes appropriate for each segment of cash holders,
(3) technical factors, such as the efficiency of the payments mechanism and the degree to which payments are offset or obviated,
(4) use of deposit balances for the purpose of compensating banks for services.

Velocities of money in the various sectors of the economy will reflect the specific relevance of these various influences in determining the demand for money balance in each sector, as well as cyclical and other differences in activity between sectors.

3. The Flow of Payments

All sectors of the economy make payments in currency as well as by check. Only purely financial transactions, including the flow of investment funds, and business-to-business transactions involve payment by check almost exclusively.

THE FLOW OF CONSUMER PAYMENTS

The level of money balances owned by households is determined largely by the same factors that determine the level of corporate balances, i.e., the volume and timing of payments and the relative attractiveness of alternative liquidity instruments.[1] Households (used here interchangeably with "consumers" and "individuals") generally try to keep bank charges at a minimum by avoiding unnecessary activity in their accounts.

In paying many current household expenditures locally, the individual usually has the choice of using either currency or check. Payments to distant points are ordinarily made by check. Households that do not own checking accounts may use postal money orders, bank money orders, or cashier's checks for long-distance (and also local) payments.[2] Any increase in the use of such means for transferring funds, like any greater use of currency, will tend to reduce the importance of personal expenditures in determining overall deposit velocity, but it will not be reflected to any significant extent in income velocity. It is not probable that changes in the use of postal and bank money orders or similar payments instruments have

---

[1] *Many of the devices adopted by business firms to improve their control over cash flows or to spread out their work loads, such as cycle billing whereby department stores space out the billing of customers over the month, automatically affect the pattern of consumer payments.*

[2] *In almost all Western European countries and in a number of other countries (about forty in all), giro transfers provide the public with a cheap and efficient means of payment as an alternative to checks. For a detailed discussion, see F. P. Thomson, Giro Credit-Transfer Systems (London, 1964).*

been large enough since the 1920's to affect demand deposit turnover ratios significantly, either in the long or in the short run. The rise in the volume of postal money orders since 1929, for instance, has roughly paralleled the increase in debits.

In the normal course of events, individuals receive currency and checks at frequent intervals, mainly in payment of wages and salaries. Investment income and Government and private transfer payments are also received by check at regular intervals. Consumers can minimize the use they make of their bank accounts (and of the resulting service charges) by cashing rather than depositing checks received. Many checks are endorsed more than once before being deposited. For example, retail stores have traditionally cashed checks for their customers. Since World War II, supermarkets have become a favorite check-cashing facility. Indeed, the volume of check cashing has assumed such proportions that, partly in an effort to avoid delays at check-out counters, most supermarket chains have established special "service booths" or "courtesy booths" to cash the checks of their customers (and, in some cases, to perform other services, such as the selling of money orders and postage stamps as well as accepting utility bill payments). By thus reducing the volume of recorded debits in relation to the actual volume of payments made, the practice of endorsing over checks tends also to reduce the importance of personal expenditures as a determinant of overall deposit turnover rates.

For lower income groups especially, accounts at thrift institutions serve as a substitute for, or supplement to, checking accounts at commercial banks. Salary and other checks received may be deposited in savings banks and savings and loan associations (as well as in savings accounts maintained at commercial banks) and withdrawals can be made as needed either in currency or in the form of cashier's checks to make payments by mail. For obvious reasons, the thrift institutions and savings departments of commercial banks normally discourage accounts of this kind which frequently fail to build up large savings balances and serve only as convenience accounts.[3] Nevertheless, some savings banks have in fairly recent years sought to attract deposits by advertising "free checks", the number of which is normally related to the size of the account.

---

[3]*"Profile of Savings Deposit Rates"*, Business Conditions (*Federal Reserve Bank of Chicago, July 1967), page 13.*

Most business transactions are paid by check. Nevertheless, business firms hold a substantial portion of the currency that is in the hands of the public, but it is held primarily for the purpose of paying wages and salaries (when they are dispensed in currency) or as till cash (in retail and service establishments), and not for making payments to other businesses or for paying taxes or dividends. Much of the remaining currency held by business establishments represents the day's cash receipts prior to their deposit in banks.

Practices and policies involved in the management of corporate cash balances are as varied as the patterns of corporate cash flows. There are innumerable variants in the basic pattern of matching the flow of payments with the flow of receipts and for bridging temporal (seasonal and cyclical) gaps in these flows. The management of corporate cash is one of the main responsibilities of the corporate treasurer. In many large corporations, a special banking division (or a similarly designated unit in the treasurer's function) is in charge of bank relations and cash management policies. Meeting check flows requires supporting bank balances, and the adequacy of collection and banking arrangements is analyzed systematically by large corporations and their bankers, with adjustments being made as needed.

It is convenient to consider business payments under two headings: those associated with current production and those representing intrafirm and other transfers between accounts of the same economic entity.

PAYMENTS RELATED TO PRODUCTION.   A large part of all payments goes for the purchase of intermediate products rather than to the agents of production. For instance, since raw materials pass through several stages of fabrication before the finished product reaches the final consumer, several transactions between individual business firms ordinarily take place; these transactions normally give rise to check payments. Similarly, when finished products are distributed to final users, several layers of distribution may be involved. As a result, the volume of check payments related to the flow of goods and services alone exceeds by several times the value of final output produced. Thus, in 1968, when total GNP amounted to $860 billion, the volume of check payments may have reached $5 trillion. The proportion of payments directly related to current output is subject to cyclical as well as to long-run fluctuations.

Any change in the composition of GNP may affect the volume of money payments required for final output. Consider, for example, the relative shift in demand away from goods in favor of services. Goods pass through several stages of fabrication and distribution, whereas services are usually sold directly to users. The growth of the service component in GNP (from 30 percent to 39 percent between 1947 and 1967) tends to reduce the volume of intermediate transactions. As a result, the total volume of payments in relation to the value of final output tends to diminish, as does also the ratio of V_t/V_y. Final output purchased or produced by the Federal Government is another example. While finished products bought by the Federal Government are paid for with United States Treasury checks chargeable to accounts with the Federal Reserve Banks and therefore excluded from reported debits, the payments for the factors of production purchased by private producers who sell the finished products to the Government as well as the related payments arising from the manufacture of intermediate products are, of course, reflected in the debit totals. Furthermore, payment of taxes by individuals and businesses may be regarded as charges against private accounts for goods and services purchased by the Government for the public benefit. Nevertheless, an increase in the Federal Government's share of the economy's output will tend to reduce debits in relation to the volume of national output. The main reason is that the Federal Government, in addition to purchasing a large volume of services, usually buys directly from producers, so that the various stages of distribution are normally eliminated.[4]

INTRACORPORATE TRANSFERS OF FUNDS. A large part of economic activity, in production and distribution, is carried out by corporations operating over extensive geographic areas, often nationwide. Total corporate purchases alone are currently equal to almost one fourth of estimated total debits at all commercial banks.[5] But a large portion of debits to corporate accounts is generated by internal activities of corporations aimed at concentrating receipts from sales, transferring them to the points of disbursement, using funds in capital and credit markets, and temporarily investing redundant funds. As a result, total corporate debits presumably represent an even larger portion of total recorded payments than the share of the corpo-

[4]*The rapid growth of the state and local government sector, absorbing 10 percent of GNP in 1965 as against only 5 percent in 1947, has also tended to retard the pos.war rise in money turnover rates since this sector is one of low velocity. In 1956, corporate income velocity, for instance, was 3.86 times state and local velocity, and even consumer velocity was 1.35 times state and local turnover. R. T. Selden, "The Postwar Rise in the Velocity of Money: A Sectoral Analysis", Journal of Finance (December 1961), page 539.*

[5]*As estimated in an annual release by the Board of Governors of the Federal Reserve System.*

40

rate sector in GNP. Management practices directed toward more efficient use of corporate cash, including systematic investment of temporarily redundant cash, tend to raise V_y over time. These practices also augment the amount of intrafirm transfers of funds in relation to the average cash balance and thus raise V_t as well.

The growing complexity of corporate structures—in part as a result of diversification of output and of mergers (in particular "conglomerate" mergers)—contributes to multiplication of separate bank accounts. The tendency to decentralize operations geographically has the same effect. There are operating advantages in separating disbursement accounts (established mainly for accounting convenience and to facilitate reporting and auditing) from collection accounts. Frequently, a corporation maintains several separate collection, disbursement, and special-purpose accounts at the same bank. National corporations (which record the bulk of corporate sales) usually have collection and/or disbursement accounts in most of the localities in which they transact business. It is not unusual for a corporation to maintain several hundreds of separate accounts, in perhaps as many banks. For national retail organizations, the number of accounts may run into the thousands. Usually the bulk of receipts is concentrated in a principal treasurer's account which is the focal point of the cash management policies of the corporation. This account may be split among several large banks located in New York City and, perhaps, in some other principal centers, even though the head office of the concern may be located elsewhere.

While the three-layer structure of collection, central treasury, and disbursement accounts is fairly common in large corporations, there also may be additional layers in each of the subsidiaries or divisional units. Instead of being concentrated at the corporate headquarters, collection of remittances may be decentralized in a number of regional centers. Similarly, disbursement checks may be drawn against a single treasurer's account, or the disbursement account may be decentralized to a varying extent. Payrolls are typically charged against local disbursement accounts, while checks in payment of raw materials or freight charges as well as for dividend and Federal tax purposes are frequently drawn against central treasury accounts.

Some corporations transfer funds from collection accounts directly to local disbursement accounts in order to minimize cross-country transfers. Other companies, to facilitate central control of cash flows or for other reasons, pass all collected funds through their principal treasury account. Systematic (even daily) withdrawal of funds from collection accounts may be accomplished by using preprinted depository transfer checks or by making proper arrangements through banks. The centralization of corporate cash can be put on a semiautomatic basis by instructing the depository bank to transfer daily collections to a central or regional account or to make such transfers when the account exceeds a specified level. Alternatively, an arrangement can be made whereby the manager of the corporation's local branch or sales office, when depositing cash and checks for collection, simultaneously deposits a draft in favor of a bank holding one of the main corporate accounts. In short, an infinite variety of corporate collection and payments patterns exists. For our purposes, it is sufficient to note that changes in these patterns affect cash balance needs, and thus V_y as well as V_t, but they do not necessarily result in proportionate changes in these two series.

The speed with which collections at, and transfers to, distant points are made influences the volume of the bank float and thus of net balances. The time element in the collection process is therefore a factor in the demand for cash balances. Intracorporate transfers of funds between banks are usually made by wire, although mails are still used for transfers to remote localities or for small amounts. The wire transfer facilities of the Federal Reserve System have always been available to all member banks to transfer large amounts of funds for the account of their customers. The establishment in 1950 of the "bank wire" system for the convenience of leading banks now (1968) links 228 banks in sixty-nine cities through a privately operated network, and thus has further aided the centralization of corporate cash balances and their rapid transfer to points of disbursement. These facilities have made money at distant points available almost instantaneously in New York or in any other money center of the country. Consequently, corporations with a relatively small number of collection (or "concentration") accounts generally arrange to have their balances wired daily to the bank handling their principal accounts. On the basis of daily summaries prepared by these banks early in the day, the corporate treasurer decides on the required transfers or other disposition of funds. The pooling of funds enables surplus balances of some operating units to offset disbursements in others. In summary, this greater mobility of balances has facilitated application of scientific principles to cash management and contributed materially to the reduction of overall cash needs of national corporations. Since each intrafirm transfer of balances from one bank to another, or from one account to another at the same bank, involves a debit (and credit) entry, thus swelling the volume of debits in relation to output and sales, techniques of money mobilization have tended to increase the volume of debits in relation to sales.

Interaccount transfers of funds are, of course, not limited to the business sector. Similar intraunit transfers take place among separate accounts maintained by government entities on the state and local levels. Wealthy individuals and professional people may also maintain multiple bank accounts for convenience or business purposes. The ultimate effect of pyramiding debits through interaccount transfers in order to reduce average cash balances carried is to increase deposit velocity in relation to income velocity.

THE FLOW OF SAVINGS AND INVESTMENT FUNDS

The savings and investment process generates large flows of payments made usually by check; the most significant exception is currency deposited by households in savings accounts. Normally, the raising of funds in capital markets, trading on stock exchanges or in over-the-counter securities, and transactions in existing real or financial assets, including portfolio adjustments, involve payments by check.

In a growing economy with large savings, the volume of financial payments generated in the process of floating and distributing new securities is large. The underwriting of these securities by syndicates of investment bankers includes pooling funds and transferring them to the ultimate borrower. Debits totaling several times the amount of financing involved may be recorded in this process and the subsequent distribution of securities. Payments originating in financial institutions are huge in relation to those involving physical outputs.[6]

The flow of savings into investment[7] may be direct (for instance, when business firms reinvest undistributed profits) or through the purchase of corporate mortgages or other income-yielding financial assets. The financial assets thus acquired (sometimes referred to as "primary" securities) represent direct claims of ultimate lenders (such as individuals) upon ultimate borrowing units. The flow of savings into investment may also involve the services of financial intermediaries who issue to ultimate lenders claims upon themselves ("secondary" or "indirect" securities), using the savings thus obtained to purchase "primary" securities issued by the ultimate borrowers.

One of the main functions of financial intermediaries is that of concentrating pools of savings and making them available to large users of funds. For organizations operating beyond a local scale, such activities often require intrafirm trans-

---

[6]*One leading financial firm recently advertised* (The Wall Street Journal, *June 26, 1968*) *that its total payments in 1967 equaled one fifth of GNP.*

[7]*Including the acquisition of financial as well as real assets.*

fers of funds similar to those described above for nonfinancial corporations. Indeed, life insurance companies, the largest of the nonbank intermediaries, use a network of local depositories and "concentration" accounts in much the same way as do nonfinancial corporations. They, too, usually maintain separate disbursement and investment accounts. A considerable volume of debits may also arise from the process of pooling savings of individuals—as in the case of mutual investment funds with their elaborate sales organizations. The widespread use of credit also generates a large flow of charges to deposit accounts (and thus reported debits) when credit is repaid.

Trading in existing claims reflects portfolio adjustments of institutional investors, nonfinancial corporations, college and similarly endowed funds, and individuals, including professional speculators. It takes place mainly on organized stock exchanges or over the counter. Various markets have different rules as to payment, and some have arrangements for offsetting payments among participants. As a result, changes in the share of transactions handled by the various markets and the channels through which these transactions take place have a definite effect on overall rates of deposit turnover as well as on the demand for cash of these participants.

Among the various types of transactions in financial assets, stock market activities have tended to generate a sufficiently large volume of debits in periods of peak activity (certainly so in the late twenties) so that they have an independent and important influence upon rates of deposit turnover, at least in the main financial centers. Indeed, it may be presumed, that throughout the 1920's trading on organized stock exchanges accounted for the bulk of financial transactions.

Indirect evidence suggests that since World War II stock market transactions have been originating a considerably smaller proportion of total payments than in the late twenties. Thus, in 1929, trading at the New York Stock Exchange was equal to nearly 120 percent of GNP; in contrast, it was less than 10 percent of GNP in each year prior to 1961, but it rose subsequently to 17 percent in 1968. In general, during the entire postwar period this percentage has been much lower than during the late twenties.[8] Similar comparisons hold for sales of corporate stock on all national exchanges and over-the-counter markets. Between 1929 and 1961, for example, stock trading on all exchanges and over-the-counter markets declined

---

[8] The New York Stock Exchange Fact Book, *1959 and 1968.*

44

in relation to GNP from 150 percent to 20 percent.[9] The value of listed corporate shares outstanding is now only about one-half as large in relation to GNP as in 1929, and the decline of the ratio of corporate bonds to GNP has been almost as large.

Individuals have increasingly relegated management of their savings to specialized institutions such as corporate pension funds, mutual funds, and trust departments of commercial banks. As a consequence, a much larger part of all corporate securities is held by financial intermediaries (one third in 1961 against one fifth in 1949 and only one fifteenth in 1929). On balance, the growing importance of institutional investors (usually looking for long-term growth) in relation to professional and occasional traders (who, especially the former, may be at least equally interested in short-term gains) is probably a principal factor in explaining the relative decline in the turnover of outstanding securities, although since the mid-1960's there has been a distinct increase in the rate of portfolio turnover by mutual funds. The relative shift from stock to bond financing and the larger amounts of private placements undoubtedly have had a similar effect.

Other types of financial transactions have not experienced the same decline relative to the general level of economic activity (measured by GNP) as corporate stocks. Compared with the late 1920's, for example, trading in Government securities (especially in Treasury bills) certainly increased when measured against almost any index of business activity. It is only since World War II that the volume of Federal Government securities has become very large by comparison with private securities, and trading in United States Treasury securities has become the single most important component of trading in financial markets. After the introduction in 1929 of the Treasury bill as a money market instrument, and the inauguration of the weekly issuance of ninety-day bills, active trading in outstanding issues began to generate a large volume of debits. The introduction of longer term bills and the widening use of coupon issues nearing maturity as a means of investing short-term funds have contributed to creating a large volume of financial debits.

There is no way of measuring the total volume of payments associated with trading in the various categories of securities or in specific financial markets and their influence on velocity. Trading in stocks and bonds is reflected in the accounts of dealers and brokers as well as of principals, such as individuals, insurance companies, and trust and pension funds, even though some part of the transactions orig-

---

[9]Report of Special Study of Securities Markets of the Securities and Exchange Commission, *88th Congress, 1st Session, House Document No. 95, Part II, page 547.*

inating from portfolio adjustments gives rise to debits (and credits) to customers' accounts with brokers rather than to the ultimate buyers' accounts at their banks.

Activities of dealers in Government securities, many of whom also make markets or act as brokers for other money market instruments, generate a large volume of debits. Dealer accounts have exceptionally high turnover rates, because average bank balances maintained by such dealers are small in relation to the volume of payments made. A special study conducted by the New York Clearing House Association shows that in February 1959 such accounts at the fourteen downtown New York banks turned over at an annual rate of 11,264 times (while accounts of members of the stock exchange and of investment bankers turned over at a rate of 300 times a year).[10] This high turnover rate reflects the peculiar way in which bank balances of Government securities dealers are used as clearing accounts. Banks make and receive numerous deliveries of securities for the account of dealers, and receive or make the corresponding payments. Such payments will exceed many times (about fifty in a working day, as the February 1959 figures show) the amount of the opening balance in the account, but will normally be about offset by an equal amount of credits. "Day loans", repayable before the close of business, also swell the volume of debits but will generally leave the closing balance unaffected, unless the transactions fail to even out by an amount large enough to require an overnight loan.

The 1950's and 1960's witnessed the emergence of new types of financial claims and the revitalization of markets in certain traditional instruments. It is quite likely that in recent years financial debits reflect to a greater degree than ever payments arising from short-term investment of surplus funds in money market instruments (not only by nonfinancial corporations but also by insurance companies, state and local governments, pension and trust funds, etc.) and foreign exchange and Eurodollar transactions rather than from stock market activity, which is a much less significant contributor to financial debits than it once was.

---

[10] *New York Clearing House Association*, An Analysis and Recommendations Prepared for the Committee on Banking and Currency: Member Bank Reserve Requirements (*Hearings before Subcommittee No. 2 of the Committee on Banking and Currency, United States House of Representatives, 86th Congress, 1st Session, on H.R. 5237, Washington, D.C., 1959), page 261.*

4. The Measurement of Velocity

In principle, the computation of transactions velocity and income velocity is simple, but the practical problems encountered in measuring and interpreting both magnitudes are many. This chapter is devoted to a discussion of the measurement of these two time series. (See Chart 2).

As is frequently the case with derived economic time series, the underlying data are collected to serve several purposes and hence do not measure perfectly the magnitudes which the two definitions of velocity require. For instance, income velocity $\left(V_y = \dfrac{GNP}{Private\ money\ supply} \right)$ is usually computed by relating *total* GNP, which includes Federal Government purchases paid with checks on United States Treasury accounts at the Federal Reserve Banks, to the *private* money supply, which excludes Treasury cash. On the other hand, the series on transactions velocity $\left(V_t = \dfrac{Debits}{Gross\ demand\ deposits} \right)$ is derived from *gross* demand deposits which include a considerable amount of duplication. There are other inconsistencies, limitations, and problems of comparability, which affect long-run comparisons but which sometimes also raise questions with regard to the significance of shorter run changes.

Exhaustive examination of the various series used to derive measures of V_y and V_t cannot be undertaken within the framework of this monograph. A discussion of the money supply series used in deriving V_y is relegated to Appendix I, and attention is there drawn to various statistical and analytical limitations of the currently used private money supply concept.

It will be observed that the V_t numerator encompasses a much greater range of payments, including intrafirm movements of funds and transactions in real and financial assets. On the other hand, the denominator is less comprehensive than that of V_y since it excludes the public's currency holdings. Both denominators exclude United States Treasury deposits. Alternative measures of V_y may be considered, and several such alternatives are discussed below.

V_y has the statistical advantage of continuity and consistency over time, even though the numerator as well as the denominator of the ratio include both estimates and reported figures. Although the two underlying series are subject to frequent

47

Chart 2. INCOME AND TRANSACTIONS VELOCITY, 1919-68

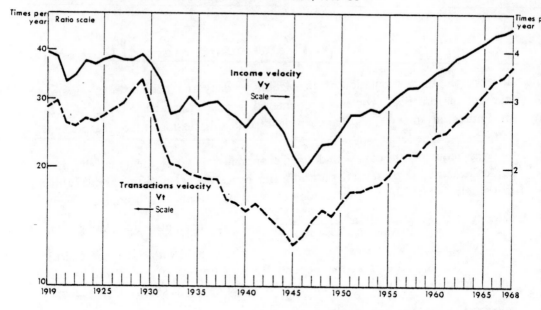

Sources: Based on data from the Board of Governors of the
Federal Reserve System; United States Department of Commerce;
and E. Oliver and A. J. Schwartz, *Currency Held by the Public, the
Banks, and the Treasury Monthly, December 1917 · December 1944,*
Technical Paper No. 4 (National Bureau of Economic Research, 1947).

revision, the continuity of coverage of the derived velocity ratios is not affected by such revisions. Not so in the case of V_t. The reporting sample of this series, which is based on reported rather than estimated data, has undergone several changes over the years in scope and coverage, and the required statistical adjustments have been changed. The various time segments must be spliced on the basis of overlap data (available in each case), and the resulting series for the entire period since World War I is, in fact, not entirely homogeneous. While broad conclusions concerning both long-run and cyclical fluctuations can be drawn from it with considerable confidence as to validity, the statistical limitations of the V_t series[1] must be kept in mind.

---

[1] *The various deposit turnover series mentioned on page 56 are published in the* Federal Reserve Bulletin.

V_y relates the current value of the aggregate final output of goods and services to the private money supply (M), disregarding all intermediate payments required to produce and distribute current output. Income velocity is not constant, either over the business cycle or over the long run. Changes in the ratio of GNP to M may reflect variations and lags in the relationships which link current output and the stock of money. Problems may also result from variations in the structure of production and distribution, changes in the efficiency of the technology of payments, and fluctuations in the amount of cash balances required to support transactions in existing real or financial assets (subsequently referred to as "financial transactions"). Indeed, the claim that the relationship between the aggregate flow of goods and services (measured by GNP) and the quantity of money is fairly stable makes at least three implicit assumptions: (1) that the average number of intermediate transactions (as a product passes through various stages of fabrication and distribution), each requiring payments between separate units, remains constant over time; (2) that aggregate demand for cash balances for all other reasons moves proportionately to that for meeting the flow of payments associated with current output; and (3) that the volume of transactions in existing assets is also proportionate to the dollar value of current output. These simplifying assumptions do not necessarily hold over time, as witnessed by the time profile of V_y and its relationship to V_t (see Chart 2).

The private money supply excludes deposits. of the Federal Government, whether held at the Federal Reserve Banks or at commercial banks (with trivial exceptions, such as accounts of disbursing agents in remote locations, where paying by check redeemable at Federal Reserve Banks would involve considerable inconvenience). The justification usually given by various students for using the private money supply to compute V_y—since there is no "official" series on income velocity —is that the level of Federal Government spending is not related in any meaningful way to the level of Treasury balances.

Two alternative measures of income velocity may be considered in an effort to remedy the deficiency of having the contribution of the Federal Government appear in the numerator of the ratio while the associated money supply is excluded from the denominator. One is to limit the velocity ratio to the private product by removing from the numerator that part of GNP which is paid for by checks drawn on United States Government accounts (V_y^1). Alternatively, United States Treasury deposits may be added to the denominator in order to establish the equivalence between the numerator and denominator in the income velocity ratio (V_y^2). Both

49

variants are shown in Chart 3.

The level of Treasury balances at commercial banks (except those rather stable amounts maintained to compensate banks for services or in a disbursement account at remote locations) reflects in the main the result of Treasury financing operations and the collection of taxes (giving rise to deposits in Tax and Loan Accounts). The argument in favor of including Treasury deposits at commercial banks thus rests not on their relationship to the level of Government spending but on their influence on the level of private deposits. These Treasury deposits occasionally show what appear to be erratic fluctuations which are transmitted to V_y, because large amounts of private deposits are transferred to the Treasury account. While these balances usually return within a relatively short period—via Treasury disbursements—to the private money supply, velocity values computed quarterly may be affected by such shifts.

It is evident in Chart 3 that inclusion of Treasury deposits in the denominator lowers the level of this variant of the velocity series (V_y^2), but cyclical variations are quite similar to those in V_y. Indeed, very short-run shifts between private and United States Treasury demand deposits do not affect quarterly totals to any great extent, and the overall result of taking into account United States Treasury deposits is to lower the velocity figures by about 4.4 percentage points.

Elimination of final United States Government purchases of goods and services from the numerator has in most years the effect of lowering the value of the velocity ratio V_y^1 by comparison with V_y. In years of rapid expansion of defense expenditures, however, such as 1951-53 and 1965-68, the velocity measure V_y^1 rose less rapidly than V_y. There is little justification for using V_y^1. It is true that, when seen from the product side of the account, such goods and services are paid by drawing checks against accounts that are excluded from the money supply. But, when viewed from the income side, all purchases by the Federal Government result in additions to private balances of the sellers of these goods and services, and thus the level of such balances is directly influenced by the amount of Government purchases. Furthermore, while the finished products purchased by the Federal Government are paid for in Treasury checks, private producers and suppliers purchase the required factors of production by drawing on their (private) accounts. Clearly in such periods a good deal of the stimulation of economic activity emanating from rising defense spending requires a considerable volume of intermediate payments. Thus, the demand for private balances is raised even though the final output is charged to Treasury balances. All intermediary sales of parts, semi-finished products, and subassemblies which move through the various stages of production also require coverage by adequate balances in private accounts and result in charges to such accounts.

Other alternative measures of income velocity may be computed by widening the concept of money to include time deposits at commercial banks, or even all categories of time and savings deposits which their owners consider to be endowed with the qualities attached to savings deposits at commercial banks. Finally, the concept of money can be enlarged still further to include various liquidity instruments used by corporations, state and local governments, and other large transactors in order to economize on cash balances, as discussed in the preceding chapter.

One such measure of income velocity (used, for instance, by Friedman and Schwartz) widens the private money supply concept to include commercial bank

Chart 3. VARIANTS OF INCOME VELOCITY, 1948–68

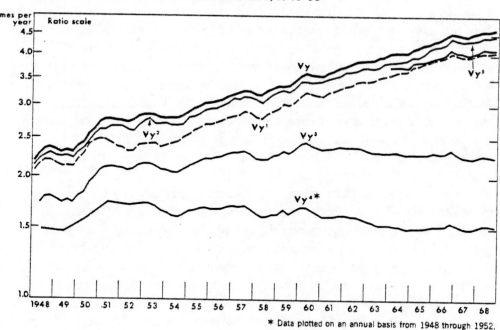

* Data plotted on an annual basis from 1948 through 1952, thereafter plotted quarterly.

Sources: Based on data from the Board of Governors of the Federal Reserve System and the United States Department of Commerce.

time deposits (V_y^2). It shows a much smaller increase since World War II because of the relatively more rapid growth of time deposits at commercial banks. In particular, following the "Accord" of 1951 commercial banks competed more actively for savings and time deposits and in the sixties succeeded in improving their position relative to thrift institutions serving primarily households. Since the war, the rate of growth of time deposits in commercial banks has substantially surpassed the rise in demand deposits. At the end of 1966, time deposits of commercial banks for the first time exceeded private demand deposits. Between 1947 and 1959, time and savings deposits at commercial banks increased at an average annual rate of 5.7 percent, compared with a rate of growth in demand deposits of only 2.5 percent. Between 1960 and 1968, time deposits grew at an average annual rate of 22.6 percent while demand deposits rose at a rate of only 4.3 percent a year. As a result, income velocity—computed as a ratio of GNP to money supply plus commercial bank time deposits—in the latter period exhibited a much lower rate of increase (whether United States Government deposits are included or not). This is true of the period from the end of World War II as a whole and especially so during the last decade when there has hardly been any increase at all.

Since the introduction of large-sized negotiable certificates of deposit (CD's) in 1961, the new instrument has been obtained and held by many corporations and other holders of large balances as a temporary investment of redundant funds, and the amounts outstanding have grown rapidly. While some funds previously invested in Treasury bills and other money market instruments were shifted into CD's, the bulk of CD's issued represents, presumably, bank liabilities previously shown as demand deposits. Furthermore, experience with CD's suggests that they may be considered a closer substitute for demand deposits than other types of time deposits. A variant of income velocity including CD's but no other types of time liabilities (V_y^3) is also shown on Chart 3.

From an analytical point of view, the logical dividing line is clearly not between demand deposits and time deposits at *commercial banks,* but rather between demand claims and time and savings deposits in *any* institution issuing such claims, whatever its legal status and the terms used might be. Indeed, if a concept broader than the private money supply is preferred, there does not seem to be any valid reason to limit it to time deposits at commercial banks alone. Time deposits of business firms are, no doubt, predominantly held with commercial banks, particularly since the banks began to issue marketable large-denomination CD's. This instrument was also successful in drawing into commercial banks a very large part of the time deposits of eleemosynary institutions and of municipalities that were formerly held at savings institutions. But for individuals—and until the emergence of CD's, for the units just cited—accounts at savings banks (in states where they exist) and in savings and loan associations constitute an alternative to commercial bank savings accounts, savings certificates, and similar instruments. The choice made by savers depends mainly on rates available and convenience of location, and only marginally on the legal status of the institution. We shall return to this issue in the following chapter. An alternative measure of income velocity, which includes time deposits at thrift institutions as well as at commercial banks in the denominator (V_y'), is also shown in Chart 3. V_y' has been declining irregularly since 1951.

TRANSACTIONS VELOCITY

Transactions velocity should ideally measure the rapidity with which the economy's total cash balances turn over. As a practical matter, it is computed as a ratio of debits (in a large but limited number of centers) to average balances in demand deposit accounts (other than interbank and United States Government accounts) since no data on currency turnover are obtainable. Yet, currency has accounted for about one fifth of the money supply in the post-World War II period as a whole. Furthermore, the share of currency in the total money supply has been subject to cyclical and long-run influences as well as to special influences arising from conditions which existed during World War II and its aftermath.[2] There is no reason to believe that efficiency in the use of currency has increased in proportion to efficiency in the use of private demand deposits; indeed, the opposite might be true.

Monthly transactions velocity data are derived as a ratio of two series, collected for a large number of "centers": debits and demand deposits (Chart 4).

The amount of debits associated with the production and distribution of one dollar's worth of final product is not constant over time. The volume of transactions in financial and real assets and of several other types of payments are only loosely associated with the level of current output. Furthermore, some payments are obviated through various kinds of compensating arrangements which in fact may or may not affect significantly the demand for cash balances. Finally, United States Treasury checks payable at Federal Reserve Banks, accounting for

---

[2] *See Appendix II.*

Chart 4. BANK DEBITS, DEMAND DEPOSITS, AND RATE OF TURNOVER IN "OUTSIDE" CENTERS, 1919-68

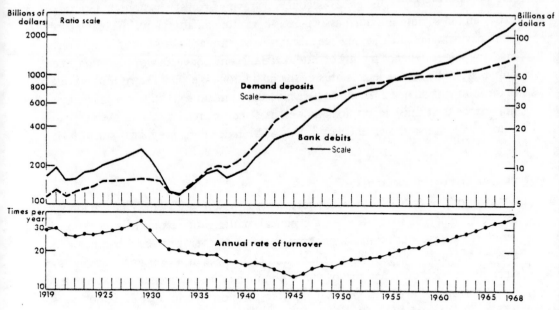

Source: Board of Governors of the Federal Reserve System.

the bulk of Federal Government payments, are not included in reported debits.

Current data on V_t have been published monthly for almost half a century in the *Federal Reserve Bulletin* (as well as in separate releases) together with debits from which they are derived. The coverage of debits has been gradually extended to include entire metropolitan areas, and estimated debits (less than one tenth of the total) were added for banks not actually in the reporting sample.[3] As a result of the most recent revisions,[4] the most inclusive series now reflects deposit activity in

---

[3]*For a detailed discussion of the various published and historical velocity and related series, see* George Garvy, Debits and Clearing Statistics and Their Use *(Board of Governors of the Federal Reserve System, revised edition, 1959), Chapter VII.*

[4]*Undertaken in 1964 and 1966. See* Federal Reserve Bulletin *(May 1965 and March 1967).*

233 standard metropolitan statistical areas; it is estimated to cover more than three fourths of all relevant debits in the country.

In terms of numbers and amounts, the overwhelming bulk of debits represents payments by check or similar forms of settlement (for example, by draft). Large payments at distant points frequently involve wire transfers. Reported debits make no distinctions with regard to the underlying transactions as long as a charge to the depositor's account arises. All transactions in real or financial assets, payments arising from the extension of credit, and the raising of funds in capital markets, as well as all transfers between separate accounts of individual economic units and the exchange of one kind of money (demand deposits) into another (currency) or into savings deposits (at the same institutions or elsewhere) or other near moneys, give rise to debits, as do also the various charges for bank services and purchases of securities through the banks. Nor are any other distinctions made between various types of deposit accounts or holder categories: special checking accounts, for instance, are pooled with regular personal and business accounts.

Published rates of turnover (seasonally adjusted) are, in fact, average rates at which the various components of private demand deposits are used; a portion of the total is turned over very intensively, while another portion, such as compensating balances maintained by business firms, is virtually at rest. Liquidity reserves and temporarily redundant funds of business firms and individuals, as well as of municipal governments and eleemosynary institutions, also have a relatively low velocity.

To simplify computations and to speed up the release of statistical data, rates of turnover are computed from gross deposits as they appear in bank records instead of from net deposits (gross deposits minus bank float). Also, bank float cannot be allocated to individual banks and, therefore, it is not possible to estimate net deposits of the banks in any standard metropolitan area or city in computing turnover rates for such areas. Actual rates of net deposit turnover are thus significantly higher than the published rates. It is likely, however, that the ratio of gross to net deposits has been sufficiently stable to justify the use of the available velocity series for at least short-run comparisons, even though at certain times transportation and/or processing delays may have resulted in fluctuations in the ratio of float to gross demand deposits. Some of the changes in the technology of collecting checks that are likely to have affected the ratio of net to gross deposits in the long run are discussed in the following chapter.

Detailed analysis of V_t for individual areas suggests that, in financial centers, payments related to securities and similar assets transactions tend to raise turnover rates, since accounts of many categories of financial firms have very high turn-over rates (Chart 5). In particular, turnover rates of demand deposits in New York City reflect to an unusual degree purely financial activities, including transactions arising from dealings on the New York Stock Exchange as well as in other securities markets.[5] This is true, though to a less extent, for other leading financial centers. As a result, since 1953 data covering the six leading financial centers[6] have been shown separately, in addition to those for New York City (which are available as far back as 1919). For certain purposes, the behavior of velocity in the separate group of financial centers is of interest. Our subsequent discussion relates, however, unless otherwise stated, only to the national series on velocity rates in the 226 "other" areas, excluding New York City and the six other financial centers. The series for the 226 centers also contains a large volume of purely financial trans-actions,[7] since some of these centers are in many respects similar to those in the six-center series.

In view of the considerable differences in turnover rates of individual accounts, plans to relate reserve requirements to deposit velocity have been advanced since the early thirties[8] when such a proposal was developed as the result of a study directed by Winfield Riefler. The Riefler proposal involved basing reserve require-ments for individual banks on total debits to total deposit accounts, subject to a

---

[5]*For a discussion of the particular factors affecting velocity in New York City, see George Garvy, op. cit., Chapters III and VII.*

[6]*Boston, Philadelphia, Chicago, Cleveland, Dallas, and San Francisco. While these centers may be regarded as the principal financial centers outside New York City for the post-World War I period as a whole, other centers are now of similar if not greater importance. To a certain degree, the choice made in 1953, when this series was initiated, was arbitrary.*

[7]*For an alternative attempt to obtain a measurement of the flow of checkbook money payments that would be as free as possible from debits originating in shifts between separate accounts of identical holders and from the transformation of demand into time deposits and financial assets of transactions, see the unpublished Ph.D. dissertation by Anthony Mach, The Institutional, Statistical and Analytical Importance of Federal Reserve Check Collections (Boston College, Graduate School, 1967). The author proposes that check collections through Federal Reserve channels be "used as a numerator in velocity studies of the transactions demand for money" (page 5). Mach found, for the period 1952-62, a stable, almost one-to-one relationship between the volume of checks collected through the Federal Reserve System (excluding Treasury checks) and "nonfinancial transactions" as estimated by McGouldrick (see page 77, f. 1). The ratio of Federal Reserve check collection to total debits fluctu-ated in the period of 1920-64, rising from 25.6 percent in 1920 to 58.6 percent in 1944 and then declining to 29.1 percent in 1964, with a strong suggestion that the changing share of purely financial debits significantly influenced this relationship.*

[8]*See Warren Smith, "Reserve Requirements in the American Monetary System", in Commission on Money and Credit, Monetary Management (Englewood Cliffs, New Jersey, 1963) and Neil H. Jacoby, "Bank Legal Reserve Requirements", Banking and Monetary Studies, ed. Deane Carson (Homewood, Illinois, 1963).*

Chart 5.   RATES OF TURNOVER OF DEMAND DEPOSITS, 1943-68

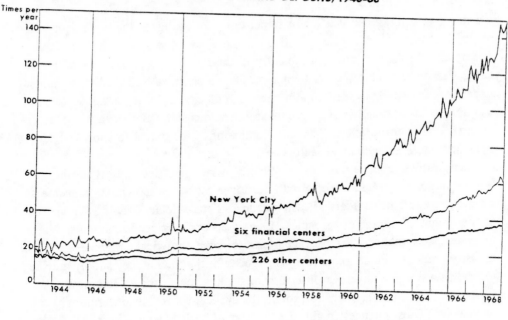

Data plotted monthly.

Source: Board of Governors of the Federal Reserve System.

maximum limit. A later proposal, made by Jacoby and Norton[9] more than a quarter of a century later, would set reserve requirements for a limited number of groups of banks (say, three or five) classified by average debits to total deposit accounts from which identifiable classes of deposit accounts involving mainly financial transactions would be eliminated. Its rationale for basing reserve requirements on deposit velocity was to use the best possible approximation of differences in the income velocity of deposits. The Federal Reserve Board would be expected to set and vary the statutory reserve ratios (not necessarily for all categories simultaneously) in the light of policy objectives.

---

[9] *Frank E. Norton and Neil H. Jacoby*, Bank Deposits and Legal Reserve Requirements (*Los Angeles, California: UCLA Graduate School of Business, 1959*).

Turnover velocity of deposits may rise because of a change in the volume of payments in relation to the volume of deposits held, or for purely technical causes. It may also fluctuate because of a change in the relative weight of various holder categories or economic sectors with typically different velocities. As one might expect, velocity differs widely among sectors. Velocity in the consumer sector, for example, is lower than in the corporate sector, and cash turns over faster at larger than at smaller corporations. Velocity fluctuations over time also show considerable differences for individual sectors.

Indeed, any aggregate measure of velocity—whether of income or transactions—is a composite of millions of money turnover ratios for individual consumers, businesses, and other holders of cash balances. Total velocity may thus be viewed as the weighted average of velocities of single accounts or economic units. When individual accounts are grouped according to some analytical principle, such as industry branches or economic regions, velocity of the total money supply may be viewed as a weighted average of a number of differing sector velocities.[10]

Structural factors may help to explain the cyclical as well as long-run behavior of velocity. Thus, changes in the distribution of cash balances between sectors and/or changes in the relative share of individual sectors with different velocities in total money payments can exert an influence on aggregate velocity. Part of the rise in total income (or transactions) velocity during periods of cyclical expansion might be explained by a greater relative gain in the volume of transactions in high-velocity sectors. Conversely, the decline in velocity, or a slower growth of velocity, during recessions might be explained in part by sharper falloffs in income (or the volume of transactions) originating in the same high-velocity sectors. Cyclical variations in aggregate turnover rates might also be explained in part by relative shifts in money holdings between sectors over the course of the cycle. The findings of one study suggest, indeed, that shifts in the relative weight of the corporate and consumer sectors are significant in explaining cyclical velocity swings.[11]

---

[10]*Studies of sector velocity are usually based on flow-of-funds estimates, from which quarterly estimates of money balance and spending (with various degrees of netting out) are available since World War II for the principal segments of the economy. Corporate data for cash and sales or revenue have also been used for measuring sector transactions velocity. See, for instance, Richard T. Selden, "The Postwar Rise in the Velocity of Money: A Sectoral Analysis", Journal of Finance (December 1961) and Paul F. McGouldrick, "A Sectoral Analysis of Velocity", Federal Reserve Bulletin (December 1962).*

[11]*See Paul F. McGouldrick, op. cit., pages 563-65.*

5. The Statistical Record

Fluctuations in velocity over the economic cycle reflect the more intensive and efficient use of money during periods of rising activity as a result in part of the higher opportunity cost of holding money. The close relationship between the level of business activity and velocity was first recognized in the early 1920's. Turnover rates of total deposits from 1870 to 1914, estimated by Carl Snyder from related data on bank clearings, clearly indicated a pattern of cyclical fluctuations during that period. For a time, an "index of the turnover of bank deposits" computed at the Federal Reserve Bank of New York was widely used as an indicator of business activity.[1] After World War II, the rate of deposit velocity continued to show a definite cyclical pattern. Measures of income velocity, available for a shorter period and on a quarterly basis only, also reflected cyclical expansions and contractions (see Chart 6).

Tables 1 and 2 demonstrate that income as well as transactions velocity has risen substantially in each period of expansion since the end of World War II, and has either declined very slightly (usually by 1 percent to 3 percent, and never by more than 5 percent) or remained essentially unchanged in each contraction. The moderate nature of velocity declines and the unchanged velocity in some periods of recession are explained, in part, by the upward trend in velocity that has characterized the whole post-World War II period and, in part, by the relative mildness of postwar recessions. Since the money supply has expanded almost continuously from the end of World War II, cyclical fluctuations in the two velocity indexes (and in the variants shown in Table 1) reflect, in the main, more rapid increases in GNP

---

[1]Carl Snyder, "Deposits Activity as a Measure of Business Activity", Review of Economics and Statistics (October 1924). See also J. W. Angell, The Behavior of Money (New York, 1936), especially Chapter IV.

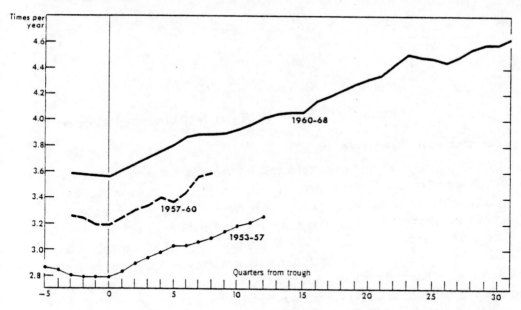

Zero line indicates troughs in business activity, as determined by
the National Bureau of Economic Research: 3rd quarter 1954, 2nd
quarter 1958, 1st quarter 1961.

Sources: Board of Governors of the Federal Reserve System
and the United States Department of Commerce.

and in the volume of debits than in private money supply or in checkbook money
in periods when the economy was expanding. In the four business contractions
since 1946, GNP declined or remained virtually unchanged, while debits fluctuated
within a very narrow range. The private (and the total) money supply as well as
demand deposits also tended to remain fairly stable, with changes in no case
exceeding 3 percent during any period of contraction.

When business activity expands, the money supply is used more intensively and
supports a proportionately greater volume of transactions. To be sure, businesses,
individuals, and governmental units tend to add to their cash holdings, partly by
borrowing additional funds from banks. At the same time, when the cost of money
is higher, they redouble their efforts to economize on balances, to find better ways

to coordinate their receipts with payments, to expedite collections, and to reduce idle funds. Since capital formation is more volatile over the cycle than other spending flows, rising activity is accompanied by a more than proportionate increase in capital expenditures and in the various activities related to their financing. Availability of new securities tends to give rise to chain reactions in portfolio adjustments, as do rising activity and price expectations associated in the equities markets. The influence of financial transactions shows up most clearly in measures of deposit velocity where, relative to GNP, the more pronounced upward thrust in debits during periods of cyclical expansion (Table 2) is due in part to increased financial activity, even in the series from which the main financial centers are eliminated.

TABLE 1

CYCLICAL CHANGES IN GROSS NATIONAL PRODUCT, MONEY SUPPLY, AND INCOME VELOCITY, 1946-69

Percentage changes between troughs and peaks

Cyclical phase	GNP	GNP adjusted*	Money supply†	Money supply‡	Income velocity (Y_1)	Income velocity (Y_2)
	(1)	(2)	(3)	(4)	(5)	(6)
1946 I —1948 IV (expansion)§	+ 34	+ 40	+ 6	+ 6	+ 26	+ 32
1948 IV—1949 IV (contraction)	− 3	− 4	− 1	0	− 3	− 3
1949 IV—1953 II (expansion)	+ 44	+ 32	+16	+15	+ 24	+ 14
1953 II —1954 III (contraction)	− 1	+ 3	+ 2	+ 3	− 2	+ 1
1954 III—1957 III (expansion)	+ 22	+ 24	+ 5	+ 4	+ 17	+ 19
1957 III—1958 II (contraction)	− 2	− 3	0	+ 1	− 2	− 3
1958 II —1960 II (expansion)	+ 15	+ 17	+ 2	+ 2	+ 13	+ 15
1960 II —1961 I (contraction)	0	− 1	+ 1	0	− 1	− 2
1961 I —1969 IV (expansion)	+ 89	+ 90	+41	+40	+ 34	+ 35
Entire period, 1946 I–1969 IV	**+385**	**+388**	**+89**	**+90**	**+157**	**+158**

Note: Cyclical phases shown between peaks and troughs, as determined by the National Bureau of Economic Research, are based on seasonally adjusted series except for column (4). Because of lack of monthly GNP figures, analysis on a monthly basis is not feasible.

*GNP minus Federal Government purchases of goods and services.

†Daily average series of private demand deposits plus currency.

‡Column (3) plus United States Government demand deposits (not seasonally adjusted).

§Instead of the 1945-IV trough for which GNP data are not available, the expansion is measured from the first quarter of 1946. Money supply for 1946-I is estimated from the end-of-the-month rather than from the daily averages series.

TABLE 2

CYCLICAL CHANGES IN DEMAND DEPOSITS, DEBITS, AND TRANSACTIONS IN VELOCITY, 1945-69*

Percentage changes, seasonally adjusted series

Cyclical phase†					Debits to demand deposits	Demand deposits adjusted‡	Transactions velocity
October	1945–November	1948	(expansion)	......	+ 63	+ 21	+ 35
November	1948–October	1949	(contraction)	....	− 4	0	− 5
October	1949–July	1953	(expansion)	......	+ 50	+ 24	+ 21
July	1953–August	1954	(contraction)	....	+ 1	+ 1	+ 1
August	1954–July	1957	(expansion)	......	+ 29	+ 8	+ 20
July	1957–April	1958	(contraction)	....	− 2	0	− 2
April	1958–May	1960	(expansion)	......	+ 20	+ 5	+ 14
May	1960–February	1961	(contraction)	....	+ 1	+ 2	0
February	1961–December	1969	(expansion)	......	+151	+ 50	+ 67
Entire period, October 1945–December 1969				....	**+821**	**+165**	**+247**

*Through 1963, in 337 centers apart from New York City and six other financial centers; from 1964 on, 226 centers. The two series have been spliced, using the ratio of 226/337 centers in 1964.

†Between peaks and troughs, as determined by the National Bureau of Economic Research.

‡Other than interbank and United States Government deposits, less cash items in process of collection.

Many of the economies in the use of money, adopted in a period of limited availability and rising costs, are not reversed in periods of easy money. The experience gained in investing excess cash in money market instruments or income-yielding savings accounts in periods when interest rates are high is not abandoned in times when the attractiveness of such investments is lessened; nor, for example, are the techniques developed to reduce mail and collection floats. Indeed, advances in the "technology" of managing money, stimulated by rate and availability factors during expansions, have a lasting effect and become a long-run influence affecting velocity.

LONG-RUN CHANGES

The admittedly deficient income and transactions velocity data for earlier periods suggest a declining trend during the nineteenth century and first decade of this century.[2] Numerous series have been constructed to study long-run trends,[3] even though for the years prior to 1919 such series have necessarily been based on somewhat doubtful assumptions and interpretations. Many of the contradictions in the conclusions reached by different investigators as to the existence and direction of a secular trend in velocity result from disagreements in defining money supply, estimating income and transactions, and time periods covered. Of course, the more the analysis is extended into the past, the more uncertain the estimates of the relevant magnitudes become.

In particular, the further we move into the past, the more the dividing line between demand and time deposits becomes blurred. Prior to the banking reform of 1933, which among other changes prohibited payment of interest on demand deposits, the difference between time and demand deposits was less sharp than in subsequent years.[4] For instance, before the establishment of the Federal Reserve System in 1913, legal reserve requirements did not distinguish between the two types of deposits. Banks and supervisory authorities, therefore, had no strong reasons for enforcing proper classification and reporting; indeed, banking statistics for these years include a large volume of unclassified deposits. Moreover, many students believe that in subsequent years, perhaps until the banking reform of 1933, a substantial volume of demand deposits was incorrectly classified as time deposits.[5] Also, the relationship between clearings (alone available prior to 1919) and debits becomes more and more uncertain the further one goes back, since origi-

[2]See, for example, Clark Warburton, "The Secular Trend in Monetary Velocity", Quarterly Journal of Economics (February 1949), and Milton Friedman and Anna J. Schwartz, A Monetary History of the United States, 1867-1960 (Princeton, New Jersey, 1963).

[3]A number of these studies are conveniently tabulated and summarized by Richard T. Selden, "Monetary Velocity in the United States", Studies in Quantity Theory of Money, ed. Milton Friedman (Chicago, 1956).

[4]Consider, for example, the following dialogue taken from the Hearing held before the United States Senate's Banking and Currency Committee in 1913 (Volume III, pages 2370-71), on the bill to establish the Federal Reserve System:
    Senator Nelson (Minnesota): "Do you issue time certificates of deposit?"
    Mr. Ingle (Vice President of a large Baltimore bank): "We issue demand certificates of deposit bearing interest...."
    Senator Nelson: "Is not that a specie of savings?"
    Mr. Ingle: "No, sir; not in our connection.... It is only in the case of a man who comes in with, say, $10,000 or $20,000, for which he has no particular use for sixty or ninety days or four months ... and feels that he ought not to let it lie in a bank earning nothing; we will then give him a demand deposit at, say, 2 or 2½ percent. I have known us to pay as much as 3 percent, but not habitually."

[5]See, for instance, Warburton, op. cit., pages 81-84.

nally clearings were reported only by large centers in which financial transactions dominated and additional cities were added only gradually.[5] Similarly, GNP estimates required to compute income velocity for the nineteenth century are based on some heroic assumptions.

The course of velocity movements since 1919 is shown in Chart 2. After a decline during the postwar recession year of 1921, both turnover rates (V_y and V_t) increased fairly steadily through 1929. Income velocity rose during the 1920's considerably slower than transactions velocity, with the result that the 1929 level of V_y just about equaled those experienced in 1919 and 1920, while V_t exceeded its post-World War I level by a wide margin. The differential behavior of the two velocity series is illustrated in Chart 7, where the ratio of V_t to V_y is plotted. The greater rise in deposit velocity in the 1920's reflects in some measure the surge in financial market activities.

During the initial years of the Great Depression, both velocity rates decreased sharply while business activity rapidly contracted. The declines continued in subsequent years (through 1945), as the economy remained excessively liquid. During these years also, the volume of deposits and money supply grew faster than business activity, whether measured by GNP or by debits. Even though production and all other aspects of business activity increased greatly during World War II, the huge volume of deposits created in the process of war financing continued to depress rates of income velocity and deposit turnover, which fell to all-time lows in 1946 and 1945, respectively. V_t declined, however, less sharply than V_y, and the ratio shown on Chart 7 rose during World War II.

As business activity continued to expand during the postwar period, the rate of growth of the money supply first slowed, then speeded up somewhat more rapidly between 1953 and 1961, and finally accelerated in the period 1961-68. While both income and deposit turnover rates increased in the post-World War II decades, the latter advanced more quickly (Chart 5) after 1953. The level of V_t was 6.5 times that of V_y in 1953, and by 1968 it was more than 8 times greater. As discussed more fully in Chapter 6, the art of money management had undergone a technological revolution since the 1950's. Greater flexibility in monetary policy and the related increased activity in the money market following the "Accord" of 1951 tended to increase the volume of financial payments in relation

---

[5]*For details, see the monograph quoted on page 54, footnote 3.*

to GNP. Rising interest rates on debits turnover and technological advances in making and collecting check payments tended to reduce the measure of money used in the denominator of both velocity ratios, but transactions velocity was further increased by additional debits generated by the investment of redundant funds in financial markets and intrafirm flows designed to increase efficiency in the use of corporate funds. For the entire period since the end of World War II, income velocity increased from 1.97 in 1946 to 4.59 in 1968, while transactions turnover rose in the same period from a low point of 12.8 in 1945 to just over 36.5 in 1968. The movements of the additional variants of V_y, shown in Chart 3, indicate quarterly changes that are not very different from those of V_y in the main series.

The rising trend of aggregate velocity characterizing the postwar decades has been broadly diffused throughout the economy. Whether one looks at the consumer sector or the business sector, manufacturing corporations or public utilities, small firms or large firms, companies producing automobiles or companies engaged in trade, the trend in income velocity during the years since the end of World War II

Chart 7. RATIO OF TRANSACTIONS VELOCITY TO INCOME VELOCITY 1919-68

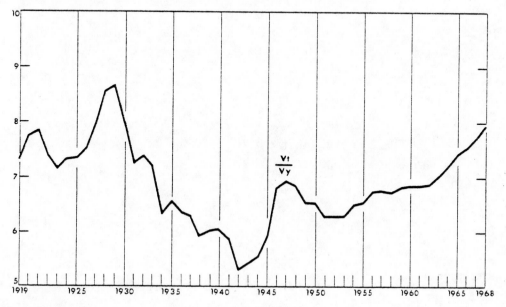

has been distinctly upward. This postwar rise does not have its roots primarily in the structural changes taking place among the different sectors of the economy. Rather, the rates of money turnover have increased for nearly all components, indicating a pervasive decline in cash balances relative to income and payments flows. Indeed, longer run structural changes (in distribution of cash holdings and in share of transactions) have worked, on balance, in the opposite direction—i.e., toward retarding the rise in velocity.[7]

The almost continuous and rapid rise in both types of measures of velocity since the end of World War II, which by the end of 1968 carried V_y to 233 percent of its level at the post-armistice trough while V_t rose 285 percent, is in striking contrast to the record of the earlier period. It is also not consistent, as we shall see in Chapter 7, with some interpretations of the forces underlying the demand for cash balances which have been advanced in recent years.

---

[7]See Paul F. McGouldrick, "A Sectoral Analysis of Velocity", Federal Reserve Bulletin (December 1962).

6. Factors Affecting Velocity

Factors affecting rates of money turnover in the long run can be grouped under four headings: first, compensating arrangements to settle payments which tend to reduce the demand for cash balances as well as the volume of debits; second, important and rapidly developing policies and arrangements designed to decrease the amount of balances required to meet a given flow of business payments; third, the related efforts of corporations to invest temporarily redundant cash; and, finally, recent developments that tend to lessen the demand for cash balances on the part of consumers.

COMPENSATING ARRANGEMENTS

Arrangements which aim at obviating the need for making payments tend to reduce the volume of check payments and the need for supporting balances. Most arrangements of this nature involve the mutual offsetting of credits and debits, usually through the intermediary of a clearing agency. Some of these clearing agreements date back to the nineteenth century; others are of relatively recent inception.

The oldest and most rudimentary form of compensation—one which does not involve any special arrangements—is used mostly in rural areas by merchants who extend credit to farmers and in turn credit their accounts as produce is purchased from them. A certain amount of netting out takes place in many interbusiness transactions. The largest volume of offsetting arises in the activities of organizations that are created specifically to clear payments stemming from certain activities which generate a large volume of transactions among a relatively small number of participants. For example, only a small proportion of the payments among brokers that result from trading securities on organized stock exchanges and/or dealings on commodity markets requires drawing checks. If these offsetting arrangements did not exist, the volume of financial payments, including a large volume of transactions in commodity futures, would constitute a much larger share of total debits than they currently do.

Arrangements to offset payments arising from trading on the New York Stock Exchange were initiated as early as 1880. Similar clearing arrangements have also been developed and perfected over the years in other exchanges and industries where frequent transactions between a limited number of firms give rise to numerous payments or credit-and-debit transactions. This process has by no means been terminated. In 1969, clearing of securities traded in the over-the-counter market was inaugurated. Trading in United States Government securities takes place over the counter rather than on organized exchanges. There is still little netting out of payments in the Government securities market and in the over-the-counter market for corporate securities.

Clearing arrangements may involve not only financial transactions but also payments among firms within certain industries. Important examples of clearing arrangements may be found in various segments of the transportation industry, such as railroads, trucking, and airlines. These compensating arrangements may be operated through banks acting as agents or on their own.

While the specific details differ, the basic principle of compensating arrangements is always the same: part of the gross payment procedure is obviated by an offsetting process among the participants. The result is that the net monetary amount of the checks written in settlement of balances is only a part, usually a small part, of the amount of the gross transactions and thus requirements for transactions balances are reduced. Consequently, offsetting arrangements tend to increase V_t. Whether on balance they increase or reduce V_y depends in each case on the alternative payments arrangements which they replace.

In contrast to transactions among members of organized exchanges and closely related business firms, netting out in payments by individuals is negligible. Important exceptions are customer balances carried by stockbrokers in those cases where securities purchases and sales and borrowing for margin purposes and related repayments (and in some instances receipts of dividends) are offset on the books of brokers so that the only resulting net differences are debit entries to customer (or broker) checking accounts.

ECONOMIZING ON CORPORATE CASH

The rise in the cost of money since the end of World War II has put pressure on corporate treasurers to reduce their cash requirements to a minimum. At the same time, demand for credit and the corresponding vigorous steps taken by commercial banks to attract funds through the introduction of additional financial instruments have offered new possibilities of earning attractive returns to holders of excess cash. The endeavors of corporate money managers to keep cash holdings shaved as closely as possible to anticipated needs, and the widespread application of scientific management principles to the utilization of cash, have tended to increase V_y. At the same time, economizing on cash balances also tends to increase the volume of financial transactions and of related debits. Since temporarily redundant funds are usually invested for very short periods, a systematic corporate policy to restrict bank balances to a minimum generates a considerable volume of financial debits as redundant funds are invested and reinvested in money market instruments, thus increasing turnover rates of corporate cash balances by increasing the volume of debits while balances are reduced.

The size of aggregate corporate cash balances is essentially determined by the volume of corporate payments. However, this relationship varies from industry to industry and from firm to firm, as well as over periods of time. Obviously, conditions differ widely among industries and individual companies, depending on seasonal patterns of production, purchasing of materials and sales of final products, billing and payments patterns, the degrees of vertical and horizontal integration, reliance on credit to meet seasonal needs, and other factors, some of which are peculiar to an industry (or even to a company) while others have wider applicability.[1] Also, liquidity needs of corporations differ extensively according to the structure of markets in which they operate as buyers and sellers, their corporate size, respective financial policies, capital structure, long-term indebtedness, current and future plant and equipment expenditures, and other factors. The corporate velocity ratio is also influenced by the need to compensate depository banks for their services and to maintain balances adequate for establishing banking relations which can assure access to credit when needed.

Modern cash management techniques originated in the 1920's, when they were but one phase of a trend toward scientific business management, by seeking new ways to employ temporarily redundant funds. Indeed, corporate funds were substantially used in financing the stock market boom of the late twenties.[2] Low interest rates in the 1930's and during World War II, however, offered limited incentives to justify maintenance of staffs required to keep redundant corporate funds continuously invested in money market instruments.

---

[1]*See Morris A. Copeland*, A Study of Moneyflows in the United States (*New York: National Bureau of Economic Research, 1952*), Chapter II, *and Richard T. Selden,* "The Postwar Rise in the Velocity of Money: A Sectoral Analysis", *Journal of Finance (December 1961).*

[2]*Loans to brokers by the weekly reporting New York City member banks "for others"—mostly corporations—rose from $579 million at the end of June 1926 to a peak of nearly $4 billion during the first part of October 1929.*

The situation changed rapidly in the postwar years, particularly after the un-pegging of rates on Government securities. At the same time, the growing prefer-ence of banks to make explicit charges, instead of requiring compensating bal-ances, to business (and other) depositors for the continuously widening range of services they offered and the general trend of corporate management to apply more scientific methods to all (including financial) aspects of corporate business stimu-lated new efforts by corporations toward a more efficient use of cash. This develop-ment was encouraged by other factors, such as the increase in corporate tax rates (with corporations regularly accumulating funds in anticipation of tax payments) and the availability of a wider range of money market instruments.

Pioneering efforts to economize on cash balances have spread rapidly through the business universe. The relatively small number of large corporations handling the bulk of business in manufacturing, public utilities, transportation, and com-munications, and increasingly in retail trade, explains why ways of handling cash developed by one became generalized fairly rapidly among other leading corpora-tions. Efforts of commercial banks in financial centers to attract corporate accounts by assisting corporate treasurers toward efficient cash management (as well as various complementary endeavors like the seminars of the American Management Association on financial management) have given added impetus in recent years to the trend toward economies in corporate cash balances. Banking concentration, especially among city banks, which eliminates the need for corporations to main-tain two or more balances in one area for goodwill reasons, accomplishes the same effect.

The trend toward greater efficiency in the use of corporate balances is portrayed in Chart 8. No series on total corporate payments is presently extant. The two principal indirect measurements available are "nonfinancial transactions" and "gross sales". The former involves complex and somewhat arbitrary estimating procedures, but it is a more inclusive measure covering all payments except those of a purely financial nature and those for existing real assets. The sales-to-money ratio is a measure of nonfinancial corporate velocity derived from accounting records. As financial transactions have undoubtedly increased more rapidly than real transactions, mainly because of the payments that are related to the investment of excess cash, total corporate payments have increased even more in relation to money holdings than is shown in either of the series.

While there is abundant evidence of corporations economizing on money hold-ings, it is also clear that overall liquidity ratios have been relatively more stable. Interest-bearing claims have been increasingly substituted for demand balances in corporate liquidity portfolios (more fully discussed in Chapter 2). The extent to which various nonmonetary liquid claims (e.g., CD's and short-term Government securities) have been substituted for cash is evident in corporate financial statements which frequently group "cash and invested cash" under a single item.

Efforts to minimize the ratio of cash holdings to corporate payments usually require systematic analysis of cash flows. However, many opportunities for husbanding cash resources can be found without undertaking such studies. Frequently, opportunities for synchronizing the flow of receipts and payments are quite obvious and cash needs can be reduced by making use of the funds in duplicate or little-used bank accounts. Many internal corporate policies have been

Chart 8.   MEASURES OF THE RELATIONSHIP BETWEEN MONEY PAYMENTS AND CASH HOLDINGS OF NONFINANCIAL CORPORATIONS

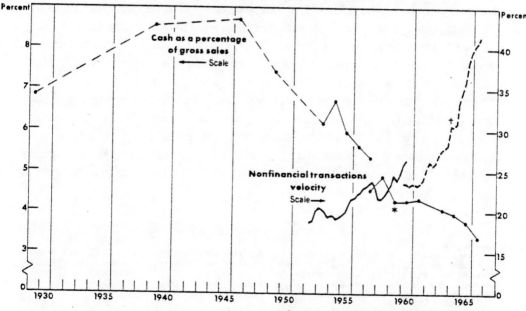

* Beginning in 1958, "business receipts" were substituted for "gross sales" which are no longer reported.

+ New series--prepared by Paul F. McGouldrick, formerly of the Board of Governors of the Federal Reserve System-- beginning in 1960.

Sources: Board of Governors of the Federal Reserve System and the Internal Revenue Service.

developed which make executives conscious of the need to economize on cash and aware of the opportunities for doing so.

Systematic analysis and the projection of corporation cash flows are not new developments,[3] but their use has become generalized only since World War II. An increasing number of corporations are now using cash budgets which, in some cases, are prepared for several years in advance but are frequently reviewed and revised for the near term.[4] Such budgeting involves relating cash needs to projected levels of sales and capital expenditures under alternative sets of assumptions. Execution of a cash budget requires close centralized control over cash flows and resources.

An important aspect of corporate cash management concerns efforts to reduce float, especially mail float. One means of reducing mail float and the volume of uncollected balances is the decentralization of remittance collections (the establishment of regional collection accounts reduces mailing time). Decentralization, together with the operation of lockbox systems, has substantially reduced mail float for large national corporations. The lockbox system involves the interception of checks at United States post offices and their channeling into collection areas as near to their point of origin as economically feasible. A firm that uses this system instructs its customers in a given area to mail remittances to a specific post office box address.[5] The depository bank then makes frequent pickups from this lockbox. Checks are immediately processed for collection, and duplicates (on microfilm or detached stubs) are forwarded to the corporation's home office for accounting purposes. An East Coast company, for example, whose billings in California would normally result in remittances being sent east and then returned to California for collection, could—by using the lockbox system—have their billings paid to a post

[3] Alfred Sloan, recounting his many years with General Motors, states that, in 1922, "We began calculating a month ahead what our cash would be each day of the month. . . . Against this projected curve we compared each day the corporation's actual cash balances. . . . By reducing our cash balances in banks, this system enabled us to invest the excess cash, principally in short-term government securities." My Years with General Motors (New York, 1963), page 123.

[4] For detailed discussion, see Robert W. Johnson, Financial Management (3rd ed.; Boston, 1966), Chapter 5, and J. Robert Lindsay and Arnold W. Sametz, Financial Management: An Analytical Approach (revised ed.; Homewood, Illinois, 1967), Chapters 8, 9, and 10. See also: Roger M. Pegram, "How Banking Serves the National Account", The Conference Board Record (May 1968), Kalman J. Cohen and Frederick G. Hammer, "Deposit Turnover, Innovations and Bank Profitability", The Banker's Magazine (Spring 1968), and Paul S. Nadler, "Banks Speed Up Velocity of Money with Innovations, Hurt Themselves", American Banker (March 19, 1963).

[5] Normally, only corporations with annual sales in excess of $25 million are likely to make use of such a service.

office box address in a California city, thus eliminating the check-mailing time from the East Coast to the West Coast and back. In turn the regional depository bank periodically (daily or when balances reach a specified level) transfers collected funds by wire, according to the company's instructions.

The benefits derived from using "remittance" banking depend on the geographic pattern of collections. For a firm with national sales, remittance banking may reduce float on the average of perhaps three days, most of it through the reduction of mail float. As a result, collected balances of corporations using remittance banking or similar arrangements are increased while checkbook balances of payers remain unchanged and their bank balances are reduced more promptly than when routine procedures are used.

Efforts to reduce mail and bank float have been aided by the gradual shortening of Federal Reserve availability schedules from the early 1920's when the maximum was eight days to a two-day maximum deferment schedule established in 1951. In fact, the latter allows part of the funds collected through the Federal Reserve System to become available to banks before actual collection (this being the origin of part of the Federal Reserve float which in recent years has averaged about $2 billion). Other efforts of the System to speed up collections include arranging for armored car routes and for consolidated air shipment of checks.

Another means of reducing cash needs is the use of drafts instead of checks drawn on banks. Though employed by a number of large companies for various kinds of payments, the use of drafts is not very widespread. Funds to cover drafts need not be available in the bank on which they are drawn until the drafts are actually presented for payment, though checks should, of course, be drawn only against "good" funds available at the time of drawing on the account. Balances must be maintained to cover all checks issued, even though the issuer knows that some of them will not be promptly presented for payment. By using drafts, however, companies can reduce their working balances to the level of expected draft presentations.[6] The use of drafts by corporate treasurers also permits a greater centralization of disbursement accounts, even when such drafts are made payable "through" several banks strategically located throughout the country.

---

[6] *A case in point is the use of drafts by the American Telephone and Telegraph Company when paying its quarterly dividends. By studying the time pattern of collection of its dividend checks, A T & T concluded that significant savings could be realized by substituting drafts for checks. Instead of depositing with the paying bank an amount equal to all dividend checks, it now deposits each day only an amount calculated (on the basis of a probability model) to cover the drafts expected for presentation that day, retaining the use of funds for shareholders who delay cashing dividend drafts.*

73

Employment of temporarily redundant funds in the money market by corporations, municipal governments,[7] and others has contributed to rising postwar income velocity and, at the same time, has increased the transactions velocity of demand deposits by generating an additional and frequently large flow of financial debits.

Corporate funds available for short-term investment usually belong to one of the following broad categories: (a) accumulation of tax reserves, in particular for the quarterly payment of corporate income taxes, (b) accumulation of funds for the payment of dividends and interest and for debt repayment or amortization, (c) funds temporarily available because of the seasonal nature of sales or of certain categories of operating expenditures, (d) funds kept liquid to take advantage of attractive business opportunities (e.g., to exercise options, to make deposits on bids), (e) proceeds of long-term financing held pending disbursement in connection with investment in plant and equipment, and finally (f) general liquidity reserves, or what some analysts, following Keynes, refer to as balances held for speculative or precautionary motives. In practice, funds that are accumulated for specific use in the future are taken into account when decisions are made with regard to the amount of liquid assets and cash that a corporation may want to hold at any time to achieve the desired portfolio balance in its financial investments. Alternative business uses of such balances may involve acquisition of nonmonetary liquid assets, repayments of short-term borrowings, or extension of credit, mainly in the form of trade credit.

The range of instruments in which temporarily redundant corporate cash may be invested has become increasingly extensive (more fully discussed in Chapter 2). Some treasurers have been successful in persuading their boards of directors to lengthen the maximum maturity of approved media for the investment of temporarily surplus funds and also to lengthen the list to include even foreign securities and trade paper.

---

[7]*There is considerable evidence that so far state and local governments have been lagging in introducing scientific principles of cash management. See J. R. Aronson, "The Idle Cash Balance of State and Local Governments: An Economic Problem of National Concern", Journal of Finance (June 1968), pages 499-508.*

Aronson's estimates, derived from an inventory approach model, are based on a single year's (1962) data, aggregate state and local government units, and have other limitations. His conclusion that in that year two thirds or more of cash balances actually held were in excess of optimal balances should be considered as merely suggestive of the magnitudes involved for this segment which, according to flow-of-funds estimates, in recent years held about 4 to 6 percent of total cash balances.

Government securities dealers, finance companies, and other users of short-term funds have greatly contributed to spreading the knowledge, and consequently the use, of money market instruments. Thus, the widening employment of repurchase agreements has to some extent resulted from the systematic efforts of users to seek out corporations likely to be, at least intermittently, a source of money market funds. The banks, too, have promoted more sophisticated liquidity management. Indeed, banks have in some instances assumed the function of managing investment of excess corporate cash. In effect, by competing for customers in offering cash-economizing or liquidity-management services, banks tend to reduce the level of aggregate business deposits in relation to a given volume of business payments for the banking system as a whole.

On the other hand, some corporate treasurers are now taking the view that income obtainable from the investment of surplus funds and from the reduction of cash balances in general is not worth the extra effort required, and that such policies entail a risk of losing the goodwill of bankers which they may need in periods of credit shortage. The difficulties experienced by some corporations in obtaining bank loans during the stringent credit conditions of mid-1966 may have strengthened the interest of corporations in maintaining good bank relations.

The various means available to business firms, especially to national corporations, for reducing cash holdings in relation to payments and for investing temporarily redundant funds are in a large way responsible for the increased turnover rates of corporate balances (and thus, of total balances) since World War II. Due to the familiar ratchet effect, these institutional and structural developments, and the initiating forces that explain their adoption, tend to increase velocity in the long run as well as cyclically. A process put in motion by a given cause (e.g., high or rising interest rates) is not reversed once the cause disappears or its intensity diminishes. Rising money rates lead to economizing on balances but, once new techniques are developed to achieve the desired results, they become a more or less permanent feature of payment and cash management techniques.[8]

---

[8]*That the various "near moneys" have acted as money substitutes for the corporate sector can be inferred from the fact that, in about two thirds of the quarters between 1952 and mid-1966, corporate money holdings moved in an opposite direction from changes in holdings of other financial assets (Government securities, time deposits, and finance paper). See Gloria Shatto, "Money Substitutes for the Corporate Business Sector", Journal of Finance (March 1967), page 84. For a very different interpretation, see Milton Friedman and Anna J. Schwartz, A Monetary History of the United States, 1867-1960 (Princeton, New Jersey, 1963) pages 659-72.*

Longer term changes in the velocity of consumer balances reflect a variety of influences, such as: the tendency to minimize checking account activity in order to reduce service charges, the more widespread use of charge accounts and other forms of consumer credit, the recent growth of credit-card and overdraft arrangements, and the increasing attractiveness of various kinds of thrift accounts, and more recently of consumer certificates of deposit. Other developments include withholding of income taxes, union dues, payments into welfare funds, subscriptions to Blue Cross and similar plans, and deduction for systematic savings by employers. No-minimum-balance accounts and the widening practice (facilitated by the use of computers) of paying interest on savings accounts encourage depositors to reduce demand balances to a minimum. Protection offered against checks being returned for insufficient funds by automatic crediting of a depositor's account with a loan (in fact, granting overdraft facilities) or transferring of funds automatically from his savings account under prenegotiated arrangements has the same effect.

The most important influence affecting consumer money holdings since World War II is the use of credit by households. Since the 1930's, banks and other lenders have widened the range of credit facilities available to individuals for personal expenditures. The rise in per capita income certainly reinforced this trend, but perhaps even more important was the quest by banks for new outlets for funds to replace short-term business loans, which had declined sharply in importance during and after the Great Depression as a consequence of the more extensive use by corporations of internally generated funds. In response to these stimuli, the banks have increasingly advertised their consumer credit activities and have competed quite successfully with the financial institutions which specialize in this field.

The increasingly rapid proliferation of charge accounts and general credit cards has, of course, tended to encourage the use of checks as a means of settlement as well as to bring payment dates closer to income receipt dates and therefore to reduce the need for maintaining cash balances in the intermediate period. After the end of World War II, the use of credit cards issued by the major oil companies and hotel chains became fairly widespread. More recently, this form of credit has rapidly expanded into general-purpose credit cards which permit charging a very wide range of goods and services, thereby making such cards the equivalent of cash. Nor is the use of credit cards limited to United States territory; credit cards are now available for consumers to charge the purchase of goods and services while traveling abroad. Carrying a credit card—or, as is often the case, a whole collection of credit cards—makes it unnecessary for the individual to have large amounts of cash in his possession. Nor does he have to have the resources, presently or in the immediate future, to cover purchases; some bank credit cards permit the holder to "charge" a loan (equivalent to an overdraft privilege), thereby further reducing the need for cash.[9]

Indeed, more recently, a number of banks have moved in the direction of extending what amounts to limited overdraft facilities by giving customers the privilege of drawing checks without adequate covering balances. Under each of the several variants of such check credit plans, loan balances are automatically established (subject to some stipulated ceiling) when checks are presented in excess of available "good" balances, which are then subsequently amortized by periodic payments, like regular personal loans. Giving consumers access to "instant" money for any purpose tends to reduce demand for liquidity and deposit balances.[10]

Just as bank services in the personal credit field have expanded rapidly since the war, so have other sources of funds for emergencies, such as those offered by personal finance companies, credit unions, and union and company welfare funds. Medicare, Blue Cross, and other medical plans meanwhile have lessened the financial impact of sudden illness. Easy access to funds to meet unforeseen expenses and the wider availability and use of various forms of insurance to meet them reduce the need for individuals to maintain cash balances for these purposes.

The greater use of credit by consumers and the availability of emergency services on a prepaid or insurance basis have tended to reduce the need for liquidity. Unemployment insurance and other forms of social security, company supplemental unemployment benefits and retirement plans, as well as the increase in job security as a result of collective bargaining, including the spread of seniority rules, have considerably reduced the need for protection against sudden changes in income. More importantly, the absence of any severe and prolonged depression since World War II has encouraged consumer readiness to buy on credit, and thus has tended to weaken the link between cash balances and the level of spending.

---

[9]*One New York bank has named its credit card "The Everything Card". To some extent, payments charged to credit cards are business rather than personal expense; this is especially true of business entertainment and travel expenditures.*

Credit extended through bank credit card and related (including check credit) plans in September 1967 amounted to only $198 million, according to Bank Credit-Card and Check-Credit Plans (a report of the Board of Governors of the Federal Reserve System, Washington, D.C., July 1968), page 3. The development of this technique is, however, still in its early stages. In contrast, nonbank credit cards, for which comparable data are not available, generate a much smaller amount of debits and credits.

[10]*Since the account is usually credited simultaneously only with the amount required to cover the check, this arrangement increases V_t as well as V_y.*

7. Implications of Recent Changes in Velocity

The sum of the reactions of all economic units to changes in the money supply determines whether, when, and to what extent these variations cause aggregate spending to change rather than be absorbed (or reinforced) by variations in velocity. Thus, velocity reflects the economy's reaction to changes in the money supply induced by the monetary authorities, together with influences traceable to largely technical factors.

Velocity is not constant over time, as assumed in the older version of the quantity theory of money, including that formulated in the Cambridge equation; nor is it a stable function of "permanent income" or wealth alone, or so strongly dependent on one single determinant, such as interest rates, as to make possible firm projections of its behavior in the long run, and certainly not in the short run.

Variability in velocity breaks the rigid link between money and income, since changes in the money supply, however induced, may result in pushing velocity up or down rather than produce the desired effects on spending and income. Contemporary advocates of a monetary policy which would concentrate on the control of the money supply do not endorse the view of the older "crude" quantity theory of money which assumed constant velocity. But they must assume that the link between the quantity of money and the level of economic activity is stable and predictable. Thus, much effort has been expended, particularly in the period since the appearance of the earlier version of this study, in developing theories and constructing models that would establish such stable relationships with identifiable underlying forces. Researchers have also examined the behavior of velocity since the end of World War II to ascertain whether the observed rise was due to some exceptional or transitory forces which would soon spend themselves and permit velocity to level off. In particular, the question was raised whether some kind of "velocity ceiling" existed which would not likely be exceeded, at least in the foreseeable future. To some extent, views on the outlook for velocity have changed as the rise in velocity has shown no sign of abating.

As turnover rates approached the levels established in the twenties, when they were influenced by the exceptionally large volume of stock market transactions, it seemed logical to conclude that recent increases in velocity experienced in the 1950's were not sustainable. Writing in 1959, Professor Lawrence S. Ritter expressed the belief "that present limits to [income] velocity are closer to an annual rate of about 3⅓ rather than the peak of 4 times per year reached in the 1920's".[1] By 1963, with income velocity approaching a turnover rate of 4 times per annum, and showing no signs of slowing down, he observed that: "There is thus less evidence today that velocity is approaching a ceiling than there was six years ago . . . . there is probably considerable room for further advance still remaining."[2] By 1967, when velocity had surpassed the 1929 peak and stood at around 4½, Professor Ritter was willing to speculate about the probability of a velocity rate of 7 or more in 1986 and chided those who still believed that "business firms and consumers have already learned just about all there is to know about how to economize on cash balances, and that no financial innovations are likely to arise over the coming decades which will make cash conservation even more possible than it is today".[3]

The post-World War II behavior of velocity has also cast doubt on the validity of the explanation advanced by Milton Friedman and Anna Schwartz in what has been perhaps the most ambitious attempt to explain velocity changes in the framework of a broad theory of economic behavior. Friedman and Schwartz regard money merely as a "temporary abode of purchasing power"[4] rather than as fulfilling several functions that can be meaningfully distinguished for analytical purposes, as Keynes and others did. Thus, in linking the demand for money uniquely to the level of "permanent income" (measured to eliminate temporary or transitory influences), they are eclectic with regard to the proper definition of money, recog-

---

[1]*Lawrence S. Ritter, "Income Velocity and Anti-Inflationary Monetary Policy"*, American Economic Review *(March 1959), page 125. A little later, Professor Richard T. Selden concluded that ". . . it seems unlikely that aggregate velocity will long continue to rise anywhere near its recent rate, and a resumption of the prewar secular decline would not be at all surprising". "The Postwar Rise in the Velocity of Money: A Sectoral Analysis",* Journal of Finance *(December 1961), page 533.*

[2]*Lawrence S. Ritter, "The Role of Money in Keynesian Theory"*, Banking and Monetary Studies, *ed. Deane Carson (Homewood, Illinois, 1963), page 150.*

[3]*Lawrence S. Ritter, "How Fast Does Money Run?"* Economic Report *(Manufacturers Hanover Trust Company, March 1967).*

[4]*Milton Friedman and Anna J. Schwartz,* A Monetary History of the United States, 1867-1960 *(Princeton, New Jersey, 1963), pages 649-50.*

nizing that a number of claims besides currency and demand deposits may fall within this interpretation. Primarily for reasons of convenience, however, they choose to define money as currency and total (demand plus time) commercial bank deposits held by the public.[5] A major consideration underlying this choice is that prior to 1914 demand and time deposits were not separately reported on a regular and consistent basis.

Friedman and Schwartz have advanced the proposition that the long-run behavior of velocity is explained by the position of money as a "luxury good", the demand for which rises more than in proportion to increases in income. The logic of their view is simple and appealing: as economic units increase their wealth they can better afford the luxury of holding a larger portion of wealth in the form of liquidity balances. As a consequence, velocity may be expected to decline over the long run. At the same time, such a claim compels Friedman and Schwartz to search for special explanations to apply to periods when velocity failed to decline.

The data presented by Friedman and Schwartz show that income velocity of the broadly defined money supply declined from about 4.6 in 1869 to about 1.7 in 1960. Nevertheless, it is obvious from their data that the long-run decline in velocity occurred primarily in the years between 1880 and the beginning of World War I.[6] For the years before 1880 no trend is visible, though one could speculate for any number of reasons that it should have declined, nor is there any apparent trend for the period 1914 to 1929. The decline between 1929 and 1946 is readily accounted for by the unusual circumstances of the depression and the war, without recourse to the "luxury goods" hypothesis.

While the broad decline in velocity between 1880 and 1914 is no doubt related to the rise in per capita income, it is likely that institutional forces played at least as important a role. Indeed, it is possible that the rise in income is but a coverall for a number of institutional factors which interacted in this period, and perhaps in earlier times as well, to increase the demand for money. One aspect of the period from 1880 to about 1914 is of special interest. It was during these years that the commercial banking industry experienced especially rapid growth.[7] The expansion of deposits came partly at the expense of currency, which declined sub-

---

[5]*Ibid., page 649, footnote 9.*

[6]*Ibid., Chart 57, page 640.*

[7]*James Tobin termed these years "the great day for commercial banking". "The Monetary Interpretation of History, A Review Article",* American Economic Review *(June 1965), page 475.*

stantially in relation to total deposits. But perhaps equally significant the growth of commercial bank deposits coincided with the sharp relative decline of mutual savings banks as repositories of personal savings in the country as a whole even though they continued to be important repositories of financial savings in the states where they were operating. In the five years preceding 1880, mutual savings bank deposits were equal to about 70 percent of all commercial bank deposits, but by the turn of the century this share had declined to 25 percent. In great part, the relative decline of mutual savings banks (in this period) occurred because they were confined essentially to the older and slower growing North Atlantic states, but even in those states their position tended to be eroded. For the country as a whole, the inflow of savings deposits into the commercial banking system must have been very large (especially in the case of "country" banks and banks away from the Eastern Seaboard), even though the large New York City banks manifested no interest in attracting or accommodating savings deposits almost up to the beginning of World War I. As a result, at least some of the decline in velocity between 1880 and 1914 is attributable to the growing role of commercial banks as thrift institutions.

Other institutional factors operated also in the direction of causing velocity to decline. Among these other influences was the growing share of output that passed through the market place, thus increasing the need for transactions balances. The enormous expansion in the number of banking offices, particularly in the Midwest and. South, may have had a similar effect. Most important, however, were the changes taking place as a consequence of increasing urbanization and the growing significance of commerce and industry in the uses of credit. Especially for households, purchase by credit was far more important in this period (and more so in the early part of the period) than in subsequent years, at least until the decades since 1920. In agricultural regions, it was not uncommon for money to be received perhaps only once or twice a year and, then, almost immediately paid out to retire debts accumulated over the previous months. Though such practices had, of course, been more widespread in earlier periods of American history, they undoubtedly still characterized the way in which large numbers of economic units (e.g., farmers and country merchants) operated. In the newer regions of the 1880's and 1890's, where agricultural and/or mining activities dominated and where banks were relatively few, or where their credits were largely of nonmercantile sorts, it should not surprise us that velocity was quite high. Nor, if this line of reasoning is valid, need we invoke the "luxury" hypothesis to explain the subsequent decline in velocity as the nation phased out its remaining frontier regions and settled down to the building of an urban and industrial society.[8]

The post-World War II rise in velocity, conflicting as it does with their "luxury goods" hypothesis, has caused Friedman and Schwartz to advance an explanation which is based on an important aspect of changes occurring in our economy since the thirties: "Other things being the same, it is highly plausible that the fraction of their assets individuals and business enterprises wish to hold in the form of money, and also in the form of close substitutes for money, will be smaller when they look forward to a period of stable economic conditions than when they anticipate disturbed and uncertain conditions."[9] Once adjustment to a stable framework of expectations is completed after war-generated disturbances, velocity will again rise.[10]

There is, however, no need to search for special explanations. Whereas between about 1880 and 1914 commercial bank deposits grew at the expense of mutual savings bank deposits, in the fifties and early sixties the thrift "deposits" of savings and loan associations and credit unions were growing at the expense of commercial bank deposits: this time, institutional change was working against the commercial banks. If savings bank deposits and savings and loan shares are encompassed in the definition of the money supply, velocity would have declined irregularly during the entire period from 1951 on, as shown in Chart 3.

There is, indeed, a natural tendency when dealing with a long span of time to concentrate on quantifiable influences (time series) and to disregard institutional changes and influences which in various subperiods shape decisions and expectations. We can observe the importance of institutional factors when dealing with the current scene; we have to reconstruct them for past periods and try to assess their significance through statistical tests. In this process, we may miss some of what was relevant at the time but which did not find proper sediment in statistical data or even in contemporary published comment.

Econometric research into systematic relationships between money and other relevant magnitudes is, by necessity, backward directed. It labors under the handicap of inadequate data and can allow for only a limited number of structural and

---

[8]Martin R. Blyn, "Income Velocity, 1880-1920: A Regional Analysis" (unpublished manuscript).

[9]Friedman and Schwartz, op. cit., page 673.

[10]". . . one might suppose that by 1960 expectations were approaching a plateau. If this be so, if the present interpretation is right, and if the experienced degree of economic stability shows no drastic change, one might expect the rise in velocity to end and the long-term downward trend to emerge once more." Friedman and Schwartz, op. cit., page 675. One might ask why the stability expectations of the "new era" of the twenties did not produce a similar downward adjustment.

institutional influences. A very large number of econometric studies on money have been published in recent years; they have enlarged and organized our knowledge of relationships prevailing in past periods of various horizons. Most of the results of the studies are plausible, stressing the role of interest rates and some other variable(s), such as income and/or wealth. In fact, velocity (the demand for money), interest rates, and income are all correlated with general business conditions, and in earlier business-cycle research (as mentioned in Chapter 5) velocity was widely used as an indicator of the cyclical position of the economy. Supply conditions are considered in demand-for-money models only indirectly, if at all, by assuming that monetary policy is reflected in interest rates. Thus, the rate used may be presumed to reflect current monetary and fiscal policies as well as expectations with regard to them.

Students are far from being in agreement on the relevant variables for a demand-for-money function and on the stability of such a function over time. Alternative rationalizations, however, can often be supported on the basis of statistical results of substantially equal persuasiveness. The limits set for this publication would be far exceeded even if an attempt were made to review the main econometric studies on the demand for money and their assumptions and implications. This is a matter of regret, tempered only by our conviction that available data are insufficient to undertake analysis on a level of disaggregation by economic sectors which we would accept as analytically meaningful.[11]

Focusing analysis on the nexus between aggregate monetary measures of economic activity and money, i.e., velocity, rather than on the demand function of money, forces the analyst to consider the institutional environment and other influences that help to explain breaks in continuity or temporary deviations.[12]

---

[11]*Thus, for instance, a comparison of estimates based on household survey results and those prepared annually as part of the flow-of-funds estimates shows considerable differences for the crucial household sector. For 1963, a year in which such a comparison can be made, the flow-of-funds tables estimate demand deposits and currency holdings in this sector to have increased by almost twice the amount estimated on the basis of a survey sponsored by the Board of Governors ($4.3 billion versus $2.2 billion), while for total savings accounts the difference was even greater ($23.0 billion versus $10.8 billion). For the two years 1960 and 1961, the flow-of-funds figures indicate an increase for the combined holdings of money and savings accounts averaging $14.8 billion, while a survey found an increase amounting to less than half a billion dollars. See Dorothy S. Projector, Survey of Changes in Family Finances (Washington, D.C.: Board of Governors of the Federal Reserve System, 1968) Table 6. The fact that in the flow-of-funds accounts the household sector includes nonprofit institutions cannot possibly account for even a small portion of this difference.*

[12]*Such as the effect of bottlenecks in the operations of major securities exchanges and the related clearing of securities and payments for them in 1968 which was a significant influence in bulging the money supply.*

Indeed, recent developments in the payments mechanism and in the management of liquidity strongly suggest that we are at the threshold of important new developments which are likely to bring further significant changes in the relationship of money to the flow of payments. How soon these developments will alter the payments mechanism and the demand for money is still largely a matter of conjecture.

One does not have to expect, however, that our check-ridden society will shortly be succeeded by the millennium of a checkless society: even less revolutionary changes in banking are likely to have considerable implications for velocity. One can, for instance, envisage the possibility of applying the overdrafts to business accounts and more generally replacing compensating balances with explicit service charges. But, if our basic payments mechanism shifts from the use of checks to credit transfers employing electronic impulses transmitted instantaneously through a system of interconnected electronic devices, much of what has been written about the velocity of, and demand for, money will doubtless become obsolete, and the very concept of money will undergo a radical change.

In the meantime other developments affecting demand and supply factors, as well as institutional innovations relating to financial instruments and markets, are continuously changing the position of money in relation to other instruments of liquidity in the various sectors of the economy.[13] Some of these institutional factors involve legislative developments, others represent the general evolution of needs and the market response to them. The introduction of deposit insurance at commercial banks in 1933 was such a structural change, and its significance increased over time, as similar provisions were passed to insure deposits at mutual savings banks and at savings and loan associations and as the maximum limits of insurable funds were gradually raised. Regulation Q and related rulings by other supervisory authorities limiting maximum allowable interest rates provided the basis for administrative actions which from time to time have changed the competitive position of individual substitutes for money as instruments of liquidity. Some other changes resulted from competitive actions taken by individual banks

---

[13]*Professor L. Ritter, after analyzing some of these changes, has concluded that "Already the financial asset we call 'money' (currency and demand deposits) has lost ground in our evolving financial system. . . . A larger and larger superstructure of debt, credit and economic activity is being erected atop a relatively diminishing monetary base.*

"What we are likely to see, then, over the coming decades, is a financial system in which techniques of portfolio and liquidity management advance far beyond the present state of the art, in which competition intensifies between and among both borrowers and lenders, and in which 'money' as we know it today starts to lose its present characteristics and takes on new ones in their place." Bank Liquidity Reexamined (Association of Reserve City Bankers, New York, 1967), page 32.

and other depository institutions which, by permitting withdrawal of savings accounts at other-than-stated quarterly interest payment dates and by introducing daily payment of interest, increased the liquidity of savings deposits as well as the returns available on them. The period encompassing the monetary policy of war-generated constraints through the Treasury-Federal Reserve "Accord" of 1951, the growing interdependence of the world's economies and financial markets following the introduction of convertibility by the major countries in 1958, the developing of trade in dollars and of the flotation of dollar securities abroad, and finally the unprecedented long period of domestic expansion since 1961 has raised many, still unanswered, questions as to how these events will affect interest rate levels and thus the opportunity cost of holding money. We are more impressed by the potential for future change in the demand for money in the continuously evolving framework of institutional factors than by the consistency of patterns derived from time series for past periods.

The years after World War II have seen a shift in demand away from money into nonmonetary liquidity claims, as several new instruments have come into being to compete with the older instruments—such as United States Government securities (mainly Treasury bills), commercial paper, including finance company paper, and bankers' acceptances—while thrift institutions and commercial banks have made various types of time deposits more attractive to households. In the words of one researcher, "all of the elasticities [of money demand, with respect to income and interest rates] appear to have declined significantly in the postwar period as compared to the prewar years".[14] Indeed, the shift in asset-holder preference suggests not so much that cash and the near moneys are substitutes as that money is becoming an "inferior" asset in relation to money substitutes. Undoubtedly, rising interest rate levels provide much of the explanation as to why money has become an inferior asset, compared with the other liquidity instruments. But it is also clear that the far-reaching institutional changes that have taken place in corporate liquidity management since the late fifties have been a very important

[14]Thus, whereas elasticities of −.1956 and .9344 were obtained for interest rates and income, respectively, in the period 1924-41, elasticities for the period covering the fourth quarter of 1946 through the fourth quarter of 1959 declined to −.0538 and .5130. Ronald L. Teigen, "Demand and Supply Functions for Money in the United States: Some Structural Estimates", Econometrica (October 1964), pages 501-3. See also David Laidler, "The Rate of Interest and the Demand for Money—Some Empirical Evidence", The Journal of Political Economy (December 1966). For the contrary view that the demand for the money function has not changed, see Allan H. Meltzer, "The Demand for Money: The Evidence from the Time Series", The Journal of Political Economy (June 1963).

influence.[15]

The introduction of the certificate of deposit (CD) in 1961, with the simultaneous creation of a secondary market, is perhaps the most significant development since World War II in influencing the cash management policies of corporations and of other holders of large cash balances, including those of state and municipal governments, the pension funds which they sponsor, and nonprofit institutions. When the first version of this monograph appeared in 1959, it was noted that corporations "make relatively little use of time deposits . . . . since the thirties Treasury bills . . . have come to occupy a position of predominance" (page 28). Indeed, until that time corporate time deposits were unwanted at many commercial banks. Corporations and others were reluctant to use for liquidity reserves an arrangement under which funds were tied up for a fixed period of time. The introduction of the negotiable CD, however, has changed the entire picture of corporate liquidity management. Between 1959 and 1968, nonfinancial corporate cash holdings declined from $32.6 billion to $28.7 billion, short-term United States Government securities from $17.3 billion to $9.2 billion, while time deposits increased from only $1.5 billion to $25.1 billion (end-of-year figures).

Other financial innovations were less dramatic than the introduction of negotiable CD's (see Table 3). Thus, since the end of World War II, various short-term securities of Government agencies were added to the range of liquidity instruments used by corporations and others. While the Federal debt itself grew only slowly, there occurred an almost fivefold increase in United States securities issued by Federal agencies (not directly guaranteed by the United States Government), from $4 billion at the end of 1952 to more than $22 billion fifteen years later. Although not direct obligations of the United States Government, these instruments are backed by the full faith and credit of the Federal Government and thus offer substantially the same security with appreciably higher yields. In recent years, the proportion of such obligations maturing within one year has been very large.

Among private obligations, commercial paper (for which an active market existed in the years prior to 1929) increased at a spectacular pace, growing in volume from a little over $3 billion at the end of 1957 to $20.5 billion at the end of 1968. Finance company paper especially gained in significance after World

---

[15]*Interest rates were also high in the twenties (the commercial paper rate in 1929 rose to almost 6 percent) and, as Friedman and Schwartz comment, the call money market "provided an equally safe and convenient means of investing funds for short periods". Friedman and Schwartz, op. cit., page 660.*

TABLE 3

SELECTED SHORT-TERM DEBT OUTSTANDING*

Billions of dollars

Type of instrument	December 1950	December 1955	December 1960	December 1965	December 1966	December 1968
Treasury bills	13.6	22.3	39.4	60.2	64.7	75.0
Other marketable Treasury securities	38.9	38.3	34.4	33.2	40.5	33.6
Federal agency issues	1.1	2.1	4.4	9.2	13.4	13.3
Total Federal Government and agency securities	53.6	62.7	78.2	102.6	118.6	121.9
Commercial paper	0.3	2.0	4.5	9.1	13.3	20.5
Bankers' acceptances	0.4	0.6	2.0	3.4	3.6	4.4
Negotiable certificates of deposit†	—	—	—	16.1	15.7	22.8
Total other short-term debt	0.7	2.6	6.5	28.6	32.6	47.7
Grand total	54.3	65.3	84.7	131.2	151.2	169.6

*Debt maturing within one year; end-of-December figures.
†Outstandings for all weekly reporting banks on the last Wednesday of December.
Source: *Federal Reserve Bulletin*.

War II. Commercial paper has an important advantage arising from the ability of the issuer to tailor the size and maturity of each obligation to the specific needs of corporations (or of other investors) employing temporarily idle funds. Very short maturities are available, and some issuers have arrangements under which funds available for one day only can be invested in commercial paper. Similarly, some corporations have utilized repurchase agreements with Government securities dealers to obtain short-term investments that would fit their needs. In more recent years, corporations have extended liquidity management to the international money market, especially by the buying and selling of Euro-dollar deposits as well as other currencies.[16]

The decline of "redundant" uninvested funds, as accumulations of funds to meet scheduled payments and various reserves are invested (and continuously

[16]See *Fred H. Klopstock*, The Euro-dollar Market: Some Unresolved Issues *(Princeton, New Jersey, 1968), in particular page 9 ff.*

reinvested) to keep a maximum of such funds in income-yielding forms, has tended to increase the turnover velocity of demand deposit accounts. A large part of the funds which in earlier literature were not improperly referred to as "idle" has shifted into the high-turnover category, being continuously invested and reinvested in the money market until the actual need to return them into the money supply immediately prior to the date of disbursement arises.

Similarly, the range of financial assets which households in general consider practicable alternatives to holding money has widened since World War II, as per capita personal income and the backlog of savings has risen to unprecedented levels. The resulting diversification of household holdings of financial assets has also been influenced significantly by the growth of financial intermediaries supplying deposit liabilities which many households have been using as an alternative for, or as a complement to, a checking account. These institutions have increasingly offered many of the services traditionally associated with commercial banking and lately have striven to obtain legislation enabling them to enlarge the range of such services. The relative growth of these nonbank financial intermediaries in the 1950's and early 1960's was not a cyclical phenomenon; it was a characteristic of the entire period, recessions and expansions alike.[17] The increase in claims issued by financial intermediaries, to individuals particularly, is important in explaining the rising income velocity of money since World War II.

The rapid growth of thrift institutions since World War II was the result of several factors, including aggressive advertising policies.[18] Throughout the 1950's, and early 1960's, the rates paid to depositors substantially exceeded the rates commercial banks were paying on time and savings deposits; after the mid-1950's, however, the differences between these rates narrowed. Qualitative factors that enhanced the safety of savings and loan shares, and thus made them more acceptable to the public, were also important.[19] For instance, in 1950 the insurance provisions of the Federal Savings and Loan Insurance Corporation were revised, so

---

[17]David I. Fand, "Intermediary Claims and the Adequacy of Our Monetary Controls", Banking and Monetary Studies, ed. Deane Carson, pages 245-46.

[18]Edgar L. Feige, The Demand for Liquid Assets: A Temporal Cross-Section Analysis (Englewood Cliffs, New Jersey, 1964), page 19. The fact that the savings institutions were mainly involved in financing the booming residential housing market of the 1950's, where net rates of return were relatively high, must also be included in any explanation—at least as a factor permitting the payment of high returns.

[19]Tong Hun Lee, "Substitutability of Nonbank Intermediary Liabilities for Money", Journal of Finance (September 1966).

that depositors could recover a larger portion of their funds in the event of default of an insured savings and loan institution. Also, the number of savings and loan associations covered by Federal insurance increased substantially. Aware that their attractiveness depends to an appreciable extent upon their ability to endow their liabilities with the characteristics of near moneys, savings institutions normally waive any legal requirements that may exist with respect to prior withdrawal notices, and they make passbook loans almost automatically.

It is a common characteristic of developed countries that the financial assets of consumers rise more rapidly than income. While households tend to diversify their holdings of financial assets, size distribution of income, convenience, limited information, and other factors tend to channel the bulk of consumer noncontractual financial savings into intermediaries that insure deposit claims. The rapid postwar rise of consumer holdings of savings deposits at commercial and mutual savings banks and of "shares" in savings and loan associations (and even more the very rapid growth of various types of savings and similar certificates on which higher rates of return are permitted by rate regulations currently in effect) is not tantamount to an increase in the demand for money, particularly if money is regarded, as it is by Milton Friedman, as a "temporary abode of purchasing power". Like other types of financial investments, such deposits are held primarily to obtain a return, not to meet a flow of payments obligations. Indeed, given our institutional framework and prevailing patterns of household savings and financial behavior, the bulk of consumer savings automatically results in additions to financial assets which some analysts include with the money supply. As long as savings deposits remain the preferred type of consumer financial savings, and the savings ratio stays close to the level of recent years, savings deposits are likely to rise at a more rapid rate than the money supply.

The very rapid growth in the fifties of nonbank intermediaries, both absolutely and by comparison with the rather sluggish growth of commercial banks,[20] gave rise

---

[20]*Among the many articles and books on this subject are the following: J. G. Gurley and E. S. Shaw, "Financial Intermediaries and the Savings-Investment Process", Journal of Finance (May 1956); J. G. Gurley and E. S. Shaw, Money in a Theory of Finance (Washington, D. C., 1960); Warren L. Smith, "Financial Intermediaries and Monetary Controls", Quarterly Journal of Economics (November 1959); David I. Fand, "Intermediary Claims and the Adequacy of Our Monetary Controls", op. cit.; J. Aschheim, "Commercial Banks and Financial Intermediaries: Fallacies and Policy Implications", The Journal of Political Economy (February 1959); and L. S. Ritter, "The Structure of Financial Markets, Income Velocity and the Effectiveness of Monetary Policy", Schweizerische Zeitschrift für Volkswirtschaft und Statistik (September 1962). For representative selections of papers on both sides of the issue, see Chapters 12 and 13 in L. S. Ritter's Readings in Money and Banking, second ed. (Boston, 1961).*

to a debate about the significance of this development for the effectiveness of monetary policy in promoting economic stability. The question was raised, in particular, as to whether in periods of expansion the shifting of funds by the public from commercial banks (presumably from demand deposits) to intermediaries, in response to the higher interest rates offered by these institutions, offset at least partially the restrictive credit actions taken by the Federal Reserve System.

Consider a situation in which the monetary authorities decide that it is in the public interest to pursue a restrictive credit policy. Suppose further that bank reserves are just sufficient to support existing deposit liabilities and that considerations of liquidity do not permit an expansion of bank loans. Assume also that rising mortgage rates and bond yields enable the various thrift institutions to raise the rates paid on savings deposits. If individuals respond by shifting demand balances from commercial banks to, say, savings and loan associations, the narrowly defined money supply is not affected. Balances owned by individuals are merely transferred through the investment activities of savings institutions to builders, other business firms, and governmental units. With additional construction activity now made possible, the level of GNP will rise and, with the money supply unchanged, so will the rate of income (and of transactions) velocity. Similar consequences would follow a shift of deposits to savings and other time balances at commercial banks, or to savings banks, or their use for the purchase of newly issued securities or securities held by nonbank investors. The expansionary effects depend upon the nature of the shifts (e.g., reduction in currency or demand balances by households or a shift of savings balances from commercial banks to thrift institutions or into primary securities). [21] In principle, however, the various asset substitutions mentioned all permit additional credit creation and income expansion. Efforts by the monetary authorities to limit the growth in the money supply are thus thwarted to the extent velocity increases. The sharp increase in interest rates (since 1965) has lessened this problem by putting the thrift institutions, with their rather long-term asset structure and undifferentiated liabilities, at a competitive disadvantage *vis-à-vis* the commercial banks. At the same time, however, the

---

[21]*For more complete discussions, together with attempts at measuring these effects, see Donald Shelby, "Some Implications of the Growth of Financial Intermediaries", Journal of Finance (December 1958); W. L. Smith, "Financial Intermediaries and Monetary Controls", op. cit.; D. I. Fand, "Intermediary Claims and the Adequacy of Our Monetary Controls", op. cit.; and Jack M. Guttentag and Robert Lindsay, "The Uniqueness of Commercial Banks", The Journal of Political Economy (September and October 1968), which contains a useful bibliography.*

rise in interest rates, to the highest levels in a century, has led (as in 1966 and 1969) to an increase in credit flows bypassing institutions (disintermediation) which also tends to offset restrictive actions taken by the central bank.

There is no doubt that shifts of holder preferences between money and money substitutes and the related activities of financial intermediaries that cause offsetting short-run movements in velocity have not infrequently tended to delay the effectiveness of changes in monetary policy. It is now widely recognized that, in countries with a developed money market, the money supply has two dimensions: size and velocity. Fluctuations in velocity reflect and respond to changes in credit conditions and monetary policy. Greater or less degrees of credit stringency also tend to cause changes in the technical efficiency of money use. In a way, changes in velocity signal to the monetary authorities how impersonal actions on their part have affected the liquidity position of the economy as a whole, after the initial reactions to the change in monetary policy have been worked out by the various sectors and in the money-using processes.

Far from being inimical to the execution of monetary policy, changes in velocity frequently perform a useful function. At times, the monetary authorities must take massive action which may create temporary disturbances at the initial point of impact. Usually there is a time lapse before policy actions in the open market or before changes in the discount rate or reserve requirements permeate the entire credit structure. In such a situation, velocity acts as a shock absorber and helps to cushion and diffuse the initial effects of policy actions. To the extent that monetary authorities are aware of the nature and possible range of these chain reactions, changes in velocity can be taken into account when determining the magnitude and timing of a required policy action.

To sum up, the post-World War II rise in income (and transactions) velocity was the result of two processes operating in the same direction. One was the increased efficiency in the payment and clearing mechanisms, thus tending to reduce transactions balance requirements in relation to a given volume of payments. The other was the gradual transfer of business and other nonhousehold balances, excepting those required to support payments and credit, into money substitutes. The volume and diversification of money substitutes available to holders of relatively large balances expanded in response to demand, and the performance of financial markets improved in part as their size grew. At the same time, the attractiveness of savings accounts at commercial banks for temporarily redundant funds of individuals grew. Other savings depositories aggressively sought to improve their competitive positions, by offering depositors greater returns and by making savings funds easily withdrawable whenever needed. One of the landmarks of the endeavors of depository institutions other than commercial banks to persuade clients that their claims were liquid as well as profitably invested was the success of savings and loan associations in obtaining legal sanction to designate their liabilities as deposits rather than as shares (effective July 1, 1969).

Thus, since World War II funds not needed to perform a payments function—either in the market for goods and services or to compensate commercial banks for their services, including the provision of credit—were gradually shifted into income-earning liquid assets. This process was stimulated by the rise in interest rates that began after the "Accord" of 1951 and gained momentum during the long and almost uninterrupted expansion of the economy that commenced ten years later and which is continuing at this writing. Certain events tended to hasten this process, such as the introduction of marketable CD's and the offering of the "magic fives" by the United States Treasury in October 1959, which dramatically drew the attention of large groups of savers to the availability of higher returns on easily accessible marketable instruments. The learning process is not even over time, since it involves a large variety of units, each of which has a different pattern of receipts and expenditures, temporary bulges of accumulated funds, and varying liquidity needs. Moreover, the larger organizations tend to create special units to manage cash flows and the cash position, so that returns may be maximized within the constraints of the particular liquidity needs of the unit. When the current return on such operations becomes negligible or even less than the cost of the special staff involved, cyclical declines in interest rates do not necessarily result in their disbandment. But since the shift into money substitutes is encouraged and facilitated by various specialized organizations originating such instruments or providing markets for them, efforts to stimulate the use of near moneys are subject to spurts when accelerated business activity leads to tight credit conditions and associated higher interest rates. Of course, progress in technology underlying the several aspects of improvements in the payments mechanism is also uneven. Innovation in management is not more continuous, or more evenly spread over time, than in technology.

For a number of reasons, judgments about the outlook for velocity are difficult to make as the sixties draw to an end. Up to the present, the time required to process checks and the speed of transportation tended to set a definitive limit upon further potential increases in velocity, while the availability of collected balances was prerequisite for making good on a check issued. New influences are likely to become more and more important in determining the relationship between money balances and the flow of payments. One is the exploration of the feasibility of a system of instantaneous payments through the use of electric impulses. Such a large-scale, and ultimately nationwide, computerized system would revolutionize the entire payments mechanism by replacing the handling of checks with transmission signals that would activate electronic book-entry systems. A checkless, or rather less check-based, system would presumably involve some automatic extension of credit in the form of limited overdraft facilities. Under such conditions, the need to have enough cash in the bank, on which current management of cash flows and cash budgeting is based, would lose much of its meaning. The amount of money underlying that part of the payments flows which would be cleared by the new system presumably would be considerably smaller than that required to make the same amount of payments by check or currency, and the velocity of money will increase greatly. It is also conceivable that the wider use of overdrafts, only recently introduced for the household sector in the form of "ready cash" and similar plans, could spread to business accounts even before the advent of the less-cash society.[22]

The full potential of such truly revolutionary changes in the payments mechanism and the effect of the changes contemplated beyond the payments mechanism are still difficult to visualize. But some experts envisage the advent of a credit transfer system in which business firms and even households will arrange for scheduled payments from their accounts to be transferred through an automated clearings system by advising their bank of the amounts to pay, to whom, and when. One can even go one step further:

> Could the system be programmed so that for a given day's work no one had more or less in his account, taking into account inflows, than needed to cover outflows? If so, velocity would approach infinity and money supply zero. However, in any foreseeable system we would have a few billions of coin and currency and probably of demand deposits. What seems more to the point for the money manager is that no

---

[22]In a study based on data from several foreign countries in which business-account overdrafts are important ("Interpreting Monetary Statistics when Overdrafting is Prevalent", an unpublished paper), W. H. White has concluded that inclusion of unused overdraft facilities would have a negligible effect on calculations of transactions velocity (less than 1 percent for an average for various periods of several years during the late forties and early fifties). Quoted in Anand G. Chandavarkar, "Unused Bank Overdrafts: Their Implications for Monetary Analysis and Policy", IMF Staff Papers (November 1968), which also contains a useful bibliography on unused overdrafts in various countries. It is by no means certain that this conclusion would be valid for the United States if overdraft facilities became widely available to business as well as to households.

one will be holding money as a storehouse of value, a liquidity hoard or anything other than a medium of exchange. Thus, the separation of the liquidity and transaction functions of money may well force money managers to turn themselves into liquidity managers, or into near-money managers, so to speak, and entail the development of an entirely new set of tools for using the financial system to influence the economy's growth and stability. The very least that will happen to us as money managers will be some enforced rethinking of money supply theories in a computerized economy.[23]

Indeed, models and parameters derived from past experience would then become clearly useless in predicting the future behavior of money balances. The indirect effects of these contemplated changes in the payments mechanism on banking activity, credit, and the entire financial system could be significant and perhaps revolutionary. Nevertheless, we are still too far removed from the implementation of any such system for its implications on velocity and on the role of money in relation to other instruments of liquidity to be explored in a meaningful way.

[23]Tomorrow's Money as Seen Today, *remarks by George W. Mitchell, Member, Board of Governors of the Federal Reserve System, at the annual stockholders meeting of the Federal Reserve Bank of Boston, Boston, Massachusetts, October 6, 1966.*

APPENDIXES

Contents:

Appendix I:

Composition of the Money Supply

The purpose of this appendix is to examine the accuracy of the private money supply series as a measure of the means of payment available to United States residents and to those foreigners who use dollars primarily to purchase goods, services, or investments in the United States market. What appears to be a clear-cut statistical concept involves, in fact, numerous measuring problems, including fairly arbitrary decisions about the allocations of certain categories of items of a mixed character. Some broader questions, such as the relationship of money to other categories of instruments of liquidity, have been discussed in Chapters 2 and 7.

Differences of view among economists exist as to what constitutes the money supply. Some favor the narrow definition underlying the series currently published in the *Federal Reserve Bulletin* which, in fact, covers deposits held by the domestic private sectors, by state and local governments, and by all foreigners;[1] others prefer a broader concept to include, at least, commercial bank time deposits. It should be noted that, prior to the creation of the Federal Reserve System, differentiated reserve requirements in favor of time deposits did not exist and many banks did not report such deposits separately. Thus, for that period, quite arbitrary assumptions must be made in estimating the proportion of total deposits represented by demand deposits. Chapter 4 discusses this issue and also comments on the shortcomings of using the money supply which excludes United States Government deposits to compute *total* income velocity and in using *gross* deposits to compute transactions velocity.

Other issues of a technical nature are given little, if any, attention in academic literature, as it is more concerned with the functions that money performs and with demand-for-money models than with the underlying monetary statistics.[2] Little

---

[1] See "*A New Measure of the Money Supply*", Federal Reserve Bulletin (*October 1960*), *pages 1102-23; "Revision of Money Supply Series*", Federal Reserve Bulletin (*August 1962*), *pages 941-51; and "Section 1: Banks and the Monetary System*", Supplement to Banking & Monetary Statistics (*Washington, D. C., 1962*). *In these sources, a discussion of slight differences between this and the end-of-the-month series may be found.*

[2] *Indeed, hardly any detailed independent investigation has been published since Lauchlin Currie's pioneering study,* The Supply and Control of Money in the United States (*Cambridge, Massachusetts, 1934*), *in particular Chapter 3 which served as the basis for the first money supply series published by the Board of Governors of the Federal Reserve System. See, however, a forthcoming monograph by Milton Friedman and Anna J. Schwartz.*

attention has been paid outside the Federal Reserve System to the technical problems of measuring the money supply, and the descriptive material dealing with the various revisions this series has undergone over time is almost entirely confined to articles in Federal Reserve publications. Our concern here, however, is with those issues only that are directly relevant to the interpretation of velocity statistics derived from money supply data.

Currency outside banks—one of the two components of the money supply—has accounted since World War II for between 20 percent and 24 percent of the total money supply, as published in the *Federal Reserve Bulletin*. (However, in most of the years between the two world wars it accounted for a smaller proportion.) Measuring this component involves a minimum of adjustment and no timing problems. In contrast, estimating private demand deposits involves a whole set of assumptions as to timing, clearing procedures, accounting techniques, and the share of checks chargeable to private deposits in the various components of float. Moreover, adjustments in the currency component affect primarily its level rather than month-to-month changes; it is not certain that the same is true for the deposit component. Deductions made from gross demand deposits to derive adjusted private demand deposits are quite large. For example, at the end of 1968, deductions from gross demand deposits amounted to $65 billion, or close to 30 percent. Furthermore, the various adjustment items are subject to significant influences, some of which are systematic but others are erratic. Estimating or reporting errors in individual deduction items may have important effects on month-to-month changes in the residual which is a measure of the demand deposit component of the money supply series.

CURRENCY

The currency component of the private money supply is, in effect, the cumulative total of all paper money issued and not demonetized or recorded as retired from circulation (unfit notes) plus the domestic coins in circulation in the United States as estimated by the Director of the Mint. This total is adjusted for amounts held in bank vaults (including estimated amounts for nonmember banks). Account is not taken of notes lost or destroyed (in disasters or inadvertently), circulating abroad, or included in numismatic collections. The estimate of the stock of coin is based on United States Treasury estimates of coin manufactured, damaged and worn coins withdrawn from circulation, certain exports and imports, and general loss.

98

NOTES LOST OR DESTROYED. Although the proportion of coins to the total amount of currency in circulation has increased from 8 percent at the end of 1939 to 11 percent at the end of 1968, Federal Reserve notes constitute the bulk of our circulating medium.[3] A relatively small part of currency outside the Treasury and Federal Reserve Banks consists of notes in denominations of $500 or more, and there is good reason to believe that these large-denomination notes are not, in fact, used for day-by-day transactions.[4] The number of these notes has declined, as has their share in the total dollar amount of notes outside the Treasury and Federal Reserve Banks (from nearly 10 percent in 1939 to only 1.2 percent at the end of 1968). Very large denomination notes are accumulated primarily for hoarding and tax evasion purposes, here and abroad.

Available evidence suggests that the amount of currency lost and destroyed is small enough to be disregarded for most analytical purposes. Valid estimates of currency destroyed or lost can be made only for the several categories of paper currency completely retired from circulation; amounts redeemed have invariably fallen short of those shown as outstanding on Treasury or Federal Reserve System records. Experience with the retirement of paper currency issued prior to 1929 (including gold certificates) indicates that approximately ¼ percent of all notes *issued* was never presented for redemption.

CURRENCY CARRIED OR CIRCULATING ABROAD. For about one hundred years, United States currency has circulated in several foreign countries, for various periods, on almost equal footing with national notes and coins.[5] For example, in Cuba and Haiti, United States currency at times represented a considerable proportion of the circulating medium. Currently, Panama and Liberia use United States dollars and do not issue any paper currency of their own. Since data are not available to estimate the amount of dollars which circulate in several foreign countries along with or in lieu of the national currencies, no correction can be made in United States money supply data. The amounts involved are much diminished since World War II and must surely be very small in relation to circulation in the United States.

---

[3]*Including vault cash, which is not part of the money supply but which cannot be broken down into notes and coin.*

[4]*Federal Reserve Bank shipments and receipts of such notes are very small, and notes are frequently returned in near-mint condition. In fact, no notes over $100 have been printed since 1945.*

[5]*See, for instance, John P. Young,* Central American Currency and Finance *(Princeton, New Jersey, 1925).*

United States currency is also carried by travelers into Canada, Mexico, Europe, and other continents. While the bulk of both these flows is returned to the United States (by banks which specialize in exchanging dollars or by returning travelers or military personnel), the supply available domestically is reduced by amounts that are unknown and that are subject to seasonal influences. Also, there is some leakage into foreign hoards, particularly to countries with unstable currencies and/or exchange controls.[6] Indeed, in some instances, United States currency has been shipped to various countries to fill insistent demands arising, in part at least, from the dollar's status as a preferred means of hoarding and of evading taxes and foreign exchange controls.[7]

CURRENCY IN EFFECT CIRCULATING IN THE UNITED STATES. We can summarize the discussion so far by the following equation:

$$C_e = C_r - (L + A)$$

C_e = currency in effect circulating in the United States.
C_r = currency as shown in money supply statistics.
L = currency lost or destroyed.
A = currency circulating or hoarded abroad.

Currency in effect circulating in the United States consists primarily of currency in the hands of consumers and business. The bulk of business currency is presumably held by retail trade and service establishments and by employers who make wage payments in cash. It also includes currency held by the United States Government, consisting of amounts held by post offices and paymasters of the armed services. This treatment is contrary to that of demand deposits in the private money supply series which excludes demand deposits held by the United States Government (except for some disbursement accounts in remote locations of very slight importance). Since no estimates of currency destroyed or lost, or held by the United States Government, are available, and even a broader guess on "A" cannot be made, no appropriate corrections can be made in the currency component of the private money supply series, which thus contains a cumulative overstatement of unknown magnitude (for further discussion, see Appendix II).

---

[6] *In periods of acute local inflation, American and other foreign firms may use dollars to pay the salaries of their local employees.*

[7] *In a recent two-year period, for instance, Brazil received shipments of United States currency considerably in excess of $300 million.*

At least two problems are involved in interpreting the deposit component of the money supply. One concerns the treatment of deposits owned by nonresident foreigners, and the other the impact of recurrent Treasury financing operations on privately owned deposits. There is, furthermore, the technical problem of properly adjusting for collection float.

FOREIGN-OWNED DOLLARS NOT AFFECTING GNP DIRECTLY. For most countries, foreign-owned deposits present no major obstacle to determining the money supply.[8] The situation is different in the United States, since the dollar has become a reserve currency as well as the cornerstone of international monetary arrangements. Furthermore, a large part of world trade is financed and settled in dollars. The amount of dollars held by foreigners for purposes unrelated to the United States domestic economy has grown over time, especially after World War II. Yet, there is no statistical basis for eliminating such deposits from the money supply series. Indeed, coverage of foreign deposits in the money supply series has been widened in recent years: first, in 1960, to include deposits owned by foreign commercial banks and subsequently, in 1962, to include those of central banks and other foreign official institutions held by the Federal Reserve Banks. The reason given for the increased coverage was that deposits of foreign banks and those of foreign governments and official institutions may be used for investment or other expenditures in much the same way as balances of other holders.[9]

A part of the foreign deposits is related to the international role of the dollar or to foreign operations of United States corporations. This raises a number of questions, particularly because of the growth of world trade and of that part of trade which is invoiced and financed in dollars, the increased role of foreign operations of United States corporations, and the growth of the Euro-dollar market. Even though transactions in foreign-owned dollars that are not directly

[8]In some countries of Western Europe, however, foreign-owned deposits are both large and subject to substantial short-run fluctuations. In Germany and Switzerland, for instance, they have been subject in recent years to higher reserve requirements and prohibitions on earning interest. Monetary statistics of most such countries, however, show foreign deposits separately.

[9]See Federal Reserve Bulletin (October 1960), page 1103, and (August 1962), page 944. The treatment of foreign deposits in the money supply series based on daily averages differs from that in the last-Wednesday-of-the-month series. For a comparison, see ibid., page 945.

related to domestic GNP may have been relatively small in the first years after World War II, they are now significant enough to affect both money supply estimates (and thus V_r) as well as deposit activity (and thus V_t), as explained below.[10]

A considerable amount of foreign balances, including those of foreign commercial banks and corporations, is connected with the trade between the United States and other countries and thus, at least in part, to their demand for our domestic output. But other balances are held because the dollar is the leading trade and vehicle currency, and much of the trade between third countries is billed and financed in dollars.[11] The level of such balances is related to the volume of trade among foreign countries rather than to the foreign trade of the United States. Similarly, the bulk of dollar balances of foreign insurance companies and nonbank financial institutions, of trading companies, and of foreign corporations of international scope is not associated in any significant way with the volume of demand for our domestic output of goods and services.

Available statistical data on foreign-held balances are not complete. A bank may not know that certain accounts are foreign, because holders frequently give a United States address for convenience or for the purpose of concealing their identity.[12] Also, only deposits owned by "nonresident" holders are reported, a term which does not cover certain resident foreigners who use dollar balances largely, or even almost exclusively, to conduct business abroad. For example, some foreign businesses maintain in the United States a base of operations for the entire Western Hemisphere (or some other area larger than the United States), and others transact foreign business, in particular when billings are in dollars, through United States subsidiaries. Their balances do not fall into the category of "nonresident accounts".

To go a step further, most large United States corporations operate abroad, and frequently on a worldwide basis. Their domestic balances reflect to a certain extent

---

[10]*Transactions in Euro-dollars result in a large volume of reported debits since, in contrast to domestic banks, deposits of foreign banks are included with private deposits and thus affect V_t. Furthermore, a large part of Euro-dollars borrowed by United States banks through their overseas branches is transferred on a day-by-day basis, even when funds are retained for longer periods.*

[11]*Deposit accounts are also held for convenience, safety, and other reasons by nonresident workers, such as Canadians and Mexicans who cross daily into the United States to live or who come periodically for seasonal employment. Such balances may or may not be ultimately repatriated and their significance as a measure of demand for current United States output is at least uncertain. No comprehensive data on such balances are available or, in fact, obtainable.*

[12]*See Review Committee for Balance of Payments Statistics,* The Balance of Payments Statistics of the United States *(Washington, D.C., 1965), page 78.*

their foreign transactions and include foreign exchange operations and other types of transfer of funds.[13] Given the size of these activities, it would be surprising if their dollar balances and the transactions passing through these balances did not constitute an element of some significance in money supply and debits statistics.

ELIMINATION OF UNITED STATES TREASURY BALANCES. The official money supply series is confined to the private sector, because the level of United States Treasury deposits at any given time cannot be regarded as determining the level of Federal Government purchases and other payments, according to generally accepted reasoning. But the same can be said, in varying degrees, of other sectors of the economy as well.

Broadly speaking, there is an inverse relationship between Treasury deposits and the private money supply. Fluctuations in tax collections and in Government expenditures for goods and services (including transfer payments) tend to follow regular patterns which are allowed for in seasonal adjustment factors. This is not necessarily true for Treasury financing operations and other large, unusual, and irregular receipts or payments. Moreover, the size of increases in Treasury deposits resulting from financings depends on the amount of initial underwriting of new issues by commercial banks and on the time profile of the sale of securities so acquired to nonbank holders. Also, when the Treasury pays off debt held by commercial banks, the subsequent effect on the money supply depends on basic bank reserve positions and loan demand. Other recipients of payments resulting from debt retirement may use the proceeds to reduce their indebtedness to the banks or to buy bank-held securities. Rate levels and money market conditions thus influence the degree to which Treasury payments tend to restore the level of private deposits. In spite of seasonal adjustments, temporary shifts of private deposits into United States Treasury balances (and reverse flows) may and do produce short-run swings in private demand deposits (in some instances, due to the incidence of payment dates for new Government securities), which are reflected in velocity but have little or no economic significance.

---

[13]The opposite is also true: some transactions involving domestic operations, such as purchases of imported raw materials, may be charged to dollar balances of foreign subsidiaries.

FLOAT ADJUSTMENT. Problems concerning the adjustments for clearings and collection float are the result of distance and delays in processing and are technical rather than conceptual. It is, however, not certain that the present estimating techniques — which consist of deducting two separate items from gross demand deposits, namely, "cash items in process of collection" and Federal Reserve float — provide an adequate approximation of the deposit component of the money supply.

The adjustment for float, intended to eliminate the double counting of deposits, results in only a partial correction because the reported figures used do not measure the deductible items precisely.[14] On the one hand, reported (bank and Federal Reserve) float is too broad, because it includes United States Treasury and interbank checks and other items not properly chargeable to accounts included in the money supply series. Subtracting float from gross deposits produces an overadjustment by an unknown amount.[15] It should be noted that (particularly when banks send checks to correspondents rather than to Federal Reserve Banks) some part of the collection float is shown in reports filed by commercial banks as "due from banks" rather than as "cash items in process of collection".[16] Since, however, the item actually deducted from gross demand deposits is "due to banks" rather than "due from banks", the money supply tends to be overstated by the amount of float reported in the latter item.

The various shortcomings of the deposit component of the money supply are significant for short-run as well as for long-run comparisons. Being largely of an institutional nature, some of these influences change only slowly over time. Although their aggregate effect on statistical totals is not normally subject to cyclical or relatively short-run influences, significant discontinuities may occur as a result of shifts in practices or conventions, and month-to-month changes may be influenced by purely technical factors, such as bulges in float.

---

[14]*The staff of the Board of Governors feels, however, that "the residual duplication . . . does not appear large enough, nor are changes in it great enough, to impair the usefulness of the data for most analytical purposes". "Section 1: Banks and the Monetary System", Supplement to Banking & Monetary Statistics (Washington, D. C., 1962), page 7.*

[15]*Other sources of overadjustments arise from the so-called "remittance float" (bank remittances for cash letters, which are part of the Federal Reserve float) and from checks collected from banks open on Saturdays and nonnational holidays.*

[16]*According to FDIC Annual Report for 1959, page 50, there were 3,351 insured banks reporting that they had no cash items in process of collection on the June 10, 1959 call date. Nearly half of all banks with deposits of less than $2 million reported no such items. See also Hobart Carr, "Pricing Correspondent Banking Services", The Bankers Magazine, Vol. 150, No. 3 (Summer 1967).*

For a variety of reasons, part of the balances shown as demand deposits is not, in fact, available to the holders. An example of this includes those amounts held to fulfill compensating-balance requirements by businesses that borrow; such balances are significant, particularly in periods of tight money. Amounts similarly immobilized include deposits held for legal purposes, such as funds in litigation or escrow and at least part of the minimum balances in some categories of personal checking accounts. Each bank has on its ledgers a certain amount of these funds, which are small in the aggregate and tend to be fairly stable over long periods of time. Also, there is very little uniformity among banks with regard to the availability of out-of-town collections to customers. Policies vary depending on categories of depositors (corporate versus personal accounts, new versus established customers, etc.) and on internal accounting procedures. For some categories of customers, especially corporate and other large customers, compensating balances may, in effect, absorb uncollected balances. For others, mostly individual deposits, "good funds" are limited to those actually collected. For still others, Federal Reserve or less liberal collection schedules apply. Not infrequently, small depositors are not given specific information on availability and learn about collection delays only when a check is returned marked "uncollected funds".

CERTIFIED AND OFFICERS' CHECKS. Among the various components of demand deposits adjusted, "certified and officers' checks" have grown most rapidly between the end of 1957 and the end of 1968. This category includes money orders, checks issued in payment of services purchased by the bank, interest and dividend checks issued by corporate trust departments, letters of credit, and bills of exchange (the latter being directly related to foreign trade).

While deposits of individuals, partnerships, and corporations (IPC, the main component of demand deposits) fluctuate moderately from week to week, the amount of certified and officers' checks outstanding is subject to fairly sharp week-to-week changes.[17] Fluctuations in certified and officers' checks are presum-

---

[17]From August 1967 to July 1968, for instance, such changes at New York City weekly reporting banks averaged 14 percent, exceeding 20 percent in one or another direction in one of four weeks. An extreme change during this period occurred in the weeks preceding and following April 10, 1968, when the amount outstanding reached the highest level ($6,237 million), 57.2 percent and 94.4 percent higher, respectively, than on the preceding and following Wednesday. These fluctuations affect primarily weekly and end-of-the-month rather than monthly average figures.

ably in part offset by corresponding fluctuations in IPC deposits.

It is not clear which among the various components of the catch-all item "certified and officers' checks" account for the sharp increase since World War II and for the sharp week-to-week fluctuations. Indirect evidence suggests that a large part may be due to transactions in Euro-dollars, foreign exchange, and domestic securities, rather than transactions related to payments for goods and services. This is reflected by the much greater expansion in this item in New York City. IPC deposits at large member banks in New York City advanced from the end of 1946 to the end of 1968 by 60 percent, while the amount of certified and officers' checks grew by 412 percent. Outside New York City, the corresponding increases amounted to 120 and 198 percent. Between December 1957 and December 1967 alone, certified and officers' checks increased in New York City by about three times and outside New York City by only about 56 percent.

The post-World War II expansion in certified and officers' checks in New York as well as elsewhere was precipitated by two distinct developments. One is the growth of travel and foreign trade, which caused the issuance of traveler's checks and letters of credit to expand. Similarly, the larger volume of capital flotations necessitated issuance of a roughly correspondingly larger volume of certified or officers' checks, as practically all underwriting syndicate negotiations require these instruments. The same is true for settlement of balances in stock clearings and in certain over-the-counter transactions. These various items may be thought of as activized balances—i.e., means of payment "on the wing"—and are properly included with the money supply. Their volume will, of course, rise with the secularly expanding levels of trade, travel, and financial activities to which they relate. If between the ends of 1957 and 1968 they had increased at the same rate as IPC deposits, by the end of 1968 their level at member banks would have been about $5.1 billion rather than $8.6 billion.

It is likely that the relatively larger growth of certified and officers' checks also reflects another type of bank activity, which is related to managing the banks' reserve position rather than accommodating customers with checking accounts and replenishing loans. When a bank obtains Euro-dollars, the lender usually asks his bank in the United States to issue an officers' check to the borrowing bank. Repayments of Euro-dollar borrowings normally involve issuance of "due bills" which are not included in deposits. These items pass, however, through the clearing and collection process and show up in the banking statistics as cash items in process of collection (float) or "due from banks". The recent growth of Euro-dollar borrowings and of foreign exchange transactions had the fortuitous effect of reducing the level of demand deposits by unknown amounts, as shown by indirect evidence. For instance, in spite of improvements in check processing and transportation, float at New York City member banks was in 1968 more than 2½ times as large as in 1957, while gross demand deposits rose only 69 percent. At member banks outside New York City, float also rose more than gross demand deposits (126 percent, compared with 51 percent), but clearly in these banks the impact of Euro-dollar operations on float was, as one would expect, smaller. Inclusion of due bills in deductible float (and in the item "due from banks") is thus another example of the shortcomings of the money supply series, as it is impossible to sort out those collection items which are not properly chargeable to "private demand deposits adjusted", such as Treasury checks and drafts on interbank accounts. The fact that day-to-day (or week-to-week) fluctuations in due bills may at times be relatively large casts additional doubt on the analytical validity of very short-run (weekly or monthly) changes in the money supply series.

STRUCTURE OF THE MONEY SUPPLY. Holdings of money balances by the main economic sectors, such as estimates prepared quarterly in connection with flow-of-funds accounts, are rough approximations, given the inadequacy of the underlying data; data are entirely lacking for deposits that are not related to economic activity in the United States. Furthermore, it should also be clear from the discussion in Chapter 2 that it is neither conceptually nor statistically possible to split private demand deposits (and, even less, money balances of any holder group) into the "purpose" categories which have been suggested in the literature. Most balances normally perform several functions and are neither held nor administered with one specific or single purpose in mind.

For purely expository purposes, however, we shall accept the distinction between "transactions" balances, which are maintained at levels adequate to meet the expected flow of payments in the near term, and all "other" (including liquidity) balances. Transactions balances are most directly related to the current level of GNP; in recent years, they have no doubt accounted for the bulk of demand deposits.

"Other" balances held by consumers include amounts accumulated pending investment (or transfer to savings and other similar accounts), proceeds of investments liquidated, and balances held to meet scheduled payments at specific distant dates (such as taxes, insurance premiums, etc.) as well as for emergencies. Similarly, "other" business balances include funds being accumulated to meet tax, interest, and dividend payments as well as disbursements in connection with investment projects[18] (including funds raised in capital markets). Municipal governments may also hold funds in excess of immediate transactions requirements.[19] Foreign deposits may also be regarded as consisting of two parts: those held to support trade, production, distribution, and investment activities in the United States, and those held for other purposes.

At least two categories of accounts are characterized by high activity: (1) working balances of nonbank financial institutions (savings banks, savings and loan associations, and credit unions) issuing claims that holders have to convert into money (check or currency) before making payments, and (2) balances of brokers and dealers in Government and other categories of securities, as well as of investment bankers, whose GNP-connected payments are negligible in relation to payments for securities newly issued or traded. The velocity of dealer and broker balances is exceptionally high,[20] in part because end-of-day balances do not reflect the amount of additional "day" money borrowed to support such payments as those arising from clearing arrangements for securities syndicate operations (including those which may arise from underwriting) which during a day are typically a multiple of the closing balances.

WHAT DEPOSIT BALANCES?

Money supply statistics are based on bank ledger records adjusted to remove—as much as possible—double counting arising from the time interval required to collect a check after it has been deposited. It is sometimes suggested that "holder record" totals are a more appropriate basis for analysis. These data make further allowance for the time during which checks are in the mails between payers and payees and for various additional delays before a check is actually deposited for collection. They are thus lower (by an amount called "mail float") than totals in the money supply series derived from bank records.

---

[18]*Demand balances owned by mutual funds, insurance companies, and pension and other institutional investors belong in this category.*

[19]*In part because of inefficiency in cash management. See the study by J. R. Aronson quoted in footnote on page 74.*

[20]*It has not proved feasible to eliminate "financial debits" from debits statistics as proposed in 1951 in George Garvy,* The Development of Bank Debits and Clearings and Their Use in Economic Analysis *(Washington, D.C.: Board of Governors of the Federal Reserve System, 1952), page 144.*

After a check is given or mailed by the payer, and before it is posted in his account, there is usually a period when, according to bank records, the same amount appears in two different private checking accounts; this situation occurs especially when the check is mailed to a distant point. If checks are mailed to payees, their subsequent collection through the banking system could, for a variety of reasons, involve delays beyond the time normally required by the mails and processing routines at banks. First, there is a period after the payer deducts the check from his checkbook stub (and the amount involved thus ceases to be part of the effective money supply) and before it is credited to another bank account—not necessarily that of the payee—during which it is part of the mail float. After the check has been deposited, there is a second period when the amount appears simultaneously in the accounts of the two banks involved in the transaction (the so-called "bank float", allowance for which is made in estimating the deposit component of the money supply as already mentioned on page 104).

For analytical purposes, demand deposits on a holder basis may thus be structured roughly as follows:

$$D_h = D_a - F = H_t + H_o + B_t + B_o + M_t + M_o + E + N + P_t + P_o$$

D_h = holder record balances related to changes in GNP.

D_a = demand deposits adjusted.

F = mail float.

H_t, B_t, and M_t = transactions balances of households, business, and municipal governments, respectively.

H_o, B_o, and M_o = "other" balances of the same three holder groups.

E = balances of investment bankers, brokers, and dealers.

N = balances of institutions issuing nonmonetary claims.

P_t = foreign balances related to transactions in the United States.

P_o = other foreign balances, including foreign monetary reserves and other official balances.

"Technological" changes in the payments mechanism (including changes in compensating balance requirements), which in the longer run are reflected in income as well as transactions velocity, are in the main related to balances H_t, B_t, M_t, N, and P_t. Fluctuations in the mail float (F), on the other hand, may at times cause temporary divergencies in the movement of bank ledger and holder record balances.

It is not easy to arrive at a proper statistical adjustment for the time element in making payments to distant points and even locally, when mails and/or checks drawn on banks located elsewhere are involved. Since the issues are conceptual, and not only statistical, it may be useful to review them briefly. This is, indeed, another instance in which the realities of economic processes conflict with the endeavor of analysts to describe such processes within a simple framework in an attempt to measure the underlying magnitudes with adequate precision and to impute specific meaning to short-term (even monthly) changes in such magnitudes.

Whether checkbook stubs (holder records) or bank ledger balances are more pertinent in determining the behavior of various segments of the economy depends on several factors. The most important include the frequency with which bank statements are rendered, the proportion of out-of-town items to the total volume of checks deposited, bank accounting procedures, and bank policies on making out-of-town funds available to customers. The owner of a bank account can have only an educated guess as to when the checks he issued will be charged to his account. An individual, e.g., may gamble that his income-tax-check payment will not clear for several weeks. But a large corporation usually receives a daily statement from its bank, and normally it will take the size and pattern of its mail float into account in the management of its cash balance. Between these two extremes there is a wide range of behavior and procedures. Broad generalizations on the proper analytical treatment of the mail float are thus difficult to make since this term covers the entire period from the issuance of a check to its being deposited for collection, particularly as some checks in the mail float are endorsed over. Checks which recipients intend to negotiate rather than to deposit are not recorded in their holder record balances but are considered by their holders as the equivalent of cash.

The practice of endorsing checks (in some cases, several times) is not limited to households; small businessmen such as retailers, service establishments, and contractors frequently endorse checks received from customers (often checks already once or twice endorsed) to pay suppliers. In particular, many Americans make purchases by cashing or endorsing over Treasury checks. This is particularly true for nearly 3 million civilian Federal employees, more than 27 million recipients of monthly social security checks, members of the armed forces stationed within the country, and millions of regular recipients of Federal payments of one kind or another (such as checks issued in connection with various farm programs). Checks issued by state and lower level governmental units are also frequently held and spent by recipients in lieu of cash. Pay checks of corporations, particularly in cities

110

with a few large employers, play a similar role.

The mail float is increased whenever checks are endorsed over rather than deposited immediately in the payee's account. Indeed, good arguments can be made for including at least part of the mail float with each sector's cash balance as measured by holder records. Circulation of endorsed checks does not affect reported (bank ledger) totals, but it reduces the volume of debits arising from a given level of economic activity, and thus the computed velocity of demand deposits.

Both mail float and bank check float are fairly large, so that their treatment has a significant effect on the computed series on demand deposits in the money supply, particularly when comparisons over relatively short periods are involved.[21] Bank float alone (the two items shown in banking statistics as cash items in process of collection and the computed Federal Reserve float) in recent years exceeded 10 percent of reported (gross) demand deposits. However, the unknown part of checks in collection channels reported under "due from banks", rather than as cash items in process of collection, may be even larger than the item actually deducted. The mail float is thought to be larger than the items deducted as items in process of collection, but there are no adequate means of measuring it.[22] Neither total mail float nor any of its components deemed relevant can be estimated directly. Thus, estimates of holder balances are derived by making rigid assumptions with regard to the mail float, disregarding influences that might be unique for any given month.

Indeed, holder record estimates (given, for instance, in flow-of-funds accounts) are derived from bank records on the basis of certain assumptions concerning the size and movement of mail float that are quite arbitrary and kept unchanged over long periods of time.[23] One assumption involves proportionality in fluctuations of mail and items in process of collection, thus disregarding any

---

[21]For a detailed discussion of the two floats and the statistical problems of measuring them, see George Garvy, "The Float in the Flow of Funds" in The Flow-of-Funds Approach to Social Accounting, Studies in Income and Wealth (Princeton, New Jersey: National Bureau of Economic Research, 1962), Volume 26, pages 431-61.

[22]Total check float (mail float and bank float combined) was estimated to be as large as 30 percent of demand deposits (other than United States Government and foreign-owned balances) as per holder records at the end of 1957. Ibid., page 439.

[23]For instance, consumer holder record balances, as estimated in the flow-of-funds accounts, are assumed, on the basis of a complex reasoning, to be equal to their bank record balances. See ibid., page 444.

111

specific influences that may affect mail float alone. Mail delays may affect the former more severely than the latter, since a large proportion of items in bank collection channels moves by air freight and on truck routes and by other means independent of the United States postal system. Conversely, reductions in bank float resulting from the successive shortening of Federal Reserve availability schedules do not necessarily result in simultaneous and proportionate reductions of mail float.

Since only bank ledger totals can be used meaningfully for analyzing short-run changes in the demand for money, our discussion is based on the deposit series derived from bank rather than holder records.

* * *

Effective July 31, 1969, the Board of Governors of the Federal Reserve System amended its regulations to require member banks to include in officers' checks and thus gross demand deposits all transfers of Euro-dollars. As a result, beginning with this date, the understatement of the money supply stemming from these transfers (as explained in pages 106-7) was eliminated. It is estimated that the total amount of these payments averaged about $3 billion per day during the month prior to this change in the regulations; it was presumably considerably smaller at the close of 1968 when all the series used in the present study end.

Share of Currency in the Money Supply

The changing share of currency and deposits in the stock of money is of some significance in explaining variations in income velocity. Indirectly, it also affects deposit velocity. If, for instance, a larger part of household payments is made by check rather than in cash, the relative weight of household payments as a determinant of deposit velocity will increase. Absence of adequate data makes it impossible to identify the effect on velocity of shifts in the ownership composition of the two components of the money supply, but such effects must be of some importance. Also, the changing share of currency in the money supply is, no doubt, one of the factors explaining divergent movements in income velocity and the transactions velocity of demand deposits (see Charts 2 and 7).

The share of currency (paper bills and coin) in the private money supply has undergone considerable change over the years. The ratio of circulating currency to total deposits had been subject to a declining trend between the end of the Civil War to the beginning of the Great Depression. It is estimated that at the end of the Civil War the public (business firms as well as consumers) held more than $80 in currency for every $100 in total deposits at commercial banks.[1] By the time the Great Depression fell upon the country (end of 1929), only $9 in currency was held for every $100 in total deposits and $17 for every $100 of demand deposits.

The declining importance of currency in the money supply was subject to sharp reversals following the banking crisis of the early thirties and during both world wars. Bank failures and the resultant loss of confidence in the banking system provide an explanation for the strong preference for currency in the early thirties. This caused a steep rise in the ratio of currency to demand deposits from .18 at the end of 1930 to more than .32 three years later. After 1933, the ratio of currency to money supply declined again for a variety of reasons, until World War II brought about a sharp increase in the relative importance of currency and the amount of currency outstanding arose fourfold. At the end of World War II, the amount of

---

[1] *Data for 1867 through 1945 are taken from Milton Friedman and Anna J. Schwartz,* A Monetary History of the United States, 1867-1960 *(Princeton, New Jersey, 1963). As explained in Appendix I, page 100, in contrast to demand deposits, currency held by the United States Government is included in the private money supply.*

currency in the hands of the public was excessive in relation to normal demand under peacetime conditions; it declined for a few years and did not begin to grow again until 1951.[2] After 1951, and especially in the sixties, the total amount of currency in the hands of the public as well as per capita holdings increased. Yet, the initial increase was so modest that the ratio of currency to demand deposits declined and did not bottom out until the end of 1958, when $25 was held in currency for every $100 in demand deposits—considerably more, however, than the $18 held at the end of 1930. Since then, the share of currency in the money supply has been rising again,[3] gradually increasing so that in December 1968 $29 was held in currency for every $100 of deposits.

Holdings by households (including farmers and professional persons) probably account for about 80 percent of all currency in the hands of the public, and a larger part of the remainder is held by unincorporated business than by corporations.[4] A very large segment of unincorporated business consists of retail trade and service establishments, and their currency holdings are quite closely related to the level of household expenditures.

Since currency is used mostly by the household sector, it can be related to consumer outlay. In 1929-30 currency holdings in the hands of the public averaged 5 percent of consumer expenditures. By the end of World War II (1945) the percentage had increased to 22 percent. Subsequent developments, including the spreading use of charge accounts and credit cards, caused the percentage to decline to 8 percent in 1968, which was still considerably above the prewar level.

It is not easy to account for the successive changes in the currency-money

---

[2]*On a per capita basis, the story is much the same; from a level of $179 in mid-1945, per capita currency holdings declined to $157 in 1960, but by mid-1968 the 1945 level had been surpassed as per capita holdings climbed to $210.*

[3]*This development was not unique to the United States. The share of currency in the money supply (defined similarly to ours) was, for instance, higher in the United Kingdom at the end of the war than before (28 percent in 1946, compared with 26 percent in 1938). This share subsequently through 1950 readjusted downward from the high wartime levels, but climbed steadily thereafter, and at 33 percent in 1958 was considerably higher than toward the end of the thirties. Since then the ratio has remained more or less unchanged.*

[4]*Allocations of currency by major segments of the business and household sectors, based on a set of assumptions rather than on reports or samples, were made by the Board of Governors for year-end dates covering the period 1934-54, but were subsequently discontinued. "Selected Liquid Asset Holdings of Individuals and Business", Federal Reserve Bulletin (July 1955), pages 749-50. In contrast, demand deposits held by business firms exceeded household holdings in 1939 by more than 70 percent and by varying—but much smaller—margins through 1954 (less than 20 percent larger), the last year for which such estimates were published (ibid., page 750). Flow-of-funds estimates combine currency with demand deposits.*

supply ratio.[5] Nevertheless, it is possible to point to several factors that appear to have played a significant role in influencing the direction of the ratio.

For the period between the end of the Civil War and up to at least World War I, the secular decline in the currency ratio presumably bore some relation to rising levels of personal income and urbanization. Why the rise in income should have caused a shift from currency payments to check payments is not immediately obvious. The gradual decline of the largely self-sufficient agricultural sector as a source of income and growing urbanization are often considered elements in explaining the secular decline of the currency ratio.[6] Rising personal incomes have enabled households to purchase more expensive goods (more conveniently paid for by check). All in all, however, it seems best to regard the income factor, along with Cagan, as "a proxy for a host of other developments which, on balance, may work to increase the demand for deposits relative to currency".[7] Some of these developments are not directly related to income, such as the growth and better performance of the banking system and the imposition of a tax on state bank notes in 1866 which caused these banks to encourage the use of checks.

The growing use of service charges on small checking accounts after 1933 may explain in part why the currency ratio failed to return to the 1929-30 low.[8] As a consequence of the cyclical decline in the nonwage income component and because of New Deal reform legislation, the redistribution of income away from the highest quintile (the group most likely to hold large deposit balances) in favor of the lower income groups may have been another factor. Wartime dislocations, population shifts, the sharp rise in military pay, and income tax evasion con-

[5]*Phillip Cagan concluded that: "These movements cannot in the main be explained by any simple correspondence with the trends of one or two economic factors, and in this respect the currency ratio differs notably from most other monetary variables." See his* The Demand for Currency Relative to Total Money Supply *(New York: National Bureau of Economic Research, 1958), page 2. See also his* Determinants and Effects of Changes in the Stock of Money, 1875-1960 *(New York: National Bureau of Economic Research, 1965) and S. L. McDonald, "Some Factors Affecting the Increased Relative Use of Currency since 1939",* Journal of Finance *(September 1956) as well as Solomon Shapiro, "The Distribution of Deposits and Currency in the United States",* Journal of the American Statistical Association *(December 1943).*

[6]*Phillip Cagan,* Determinants and Effects of Changes in the Stock of Money, 1875-1960, *page 127. Yet, as Cagan emphasizes, urbanization may work both to increase the currency ratio (since the impersonal nature of urban buying discourages the use of checks and, more importantly, of credit) and to cause it to decline (urban life provides familiarity with the advantages of checking accounts and encourages the banking habit).*

[7]*Ibid., page 126.*

[8]*Too much emphasis should not be placed on this factor for, as Cagan points out, "the typical rate, when charged, was probably well below one half of one percent", ibid., page 123.*

tributed to the rise in the demand for currency during World War II. After the war, the changing structure of household expenditures, including the trend toward a larger volume of personal (other than domestic) services—eating out, travel, etc. —together with the ever-widening use of vending machines, is likely to have contributed to increasing average absolute amounts of currency holdings per household. The rising share of coin in currency in circulation confirms some of the explanations frequently given for higher (absolute and relative) holdings of currency, while the declining share of very large denominations ($500 and over) since the end of World War II seems to confirm the diminishing use of currency for hoarding and concealment purposes.

Taken together, available evidence suggests that the rise in the currency ratio since World War II is not evidence of an increasing demand for folding money as a means of payment but is indicative of the declining role of money as a store of value. Measured as a multiple of weeks of average disposable income per person, the amount of currency has been declining since the end of the war almost continuously.[9] The decline of currency holdings in relation to total income, average weekly earnings, and consumer expenditures is consistent with the hypothesis that the main reason for the relative increase in the share of currency in the total money supply in the recent decade or so must not be sought in a shift of preferences for holding folding rather than checkbook money for transactions purposes. Rather, demand deposits have come to include a diminishing portion of redundant and reserve ("idle") funds of business firms and individuals, which have been shifted increasingly into income-earning money market instruments and—for households —also into various kinds of savings and other time deposits.

---

[9]See George G. Kaufman, "The Demand for Currency", Staff Economic Studies (Board of Governors of the Federal Reserve System, 1966), Table 9, page 40.